ALGEBRA MADE EASY

A Practical Approach to Algebra

A practical approach to understanding general mathematical concepts. Algebra is not just about addition and subtraction; it is about your ability to reason, draw conclusions and then take action. This book presents math as a problem solving technique; a skill that we use every day of our lives and that every person needs.

Marcia Lawson

Self-published by Author

ALGEBRA MADE EASY

A Practical Approach to Algebra

Copyright© 2012 by Marcia Lawson

Self-Published by Author

All rights reserved. No part of this book may be reproduced or transmitted in any manner whatsoever without written permission except in the case of brief quotation embodied in critical articles and reviews.

Book design by Marcia Lawson

Printed in the United States of America

First Edition Printing in 2012

ISBN-13: 978-1479208074
ISBN-10: 1479208078

ALGEBRA MADE EASY
A Practical Approach to Algebra

This book serves as a roadmap for self-studying and learning basic algebra skills. The topics which required extensive review received it. The connection between concepts and their connection to real life application are highlighted.

This book also presents some important advice and suggestions for how to study and learn algebra and how to make the connection to life situations. Most students learn the concepts but not many learn how to make the connection between what they have been taught and what they do on a daily basis. This book attempts to change that by presenting applicable situations utilizing the concepts taught. First the concept is taught then the opportunity to apply it.

There are five unit tests which are designed to test student's mastery of groups of concepts. Math is not mutually exclusive therefore once you learn a concept you should expect to see it again. For example, once you learned that A,E,I,O,U are vowels you are not told that every time you come across them, however you are expected to know that they are when you encounter them. The same is true with math, once you learn a concept for example PEMDAS, you will not be taught it every time you come across it however you are expected to know it and how to apply it.

This book explains math in a very straight forward and conventional manner. This book should be used as supplemental material to enhance your math learning experience. Concepts are presented in small chunks and are built upon with each new concept.

Unless otherwise stated, the solutions and answers to the exercises are located at the back of the text.

ALGEBRA MADE EASY
Contents

Preface

Unit 1: **How to Succeed**
Learning Objectives and Introduction

Unit 2: **Real Numbers**
Real numbers, Expanded and Standard Notations

Unit 3 **The Number system**
Classification of Numbers

Unit 4: **Operation on Real Numbers**
Addition, Subtraction, Multiplication & Division of Numbers

Unit 5: **Negative Numbers**
Adding and Subtracting Negative Numbers

Unit 6: **Properties of Real Numbers**
Associated, Commutative and Distributive Properties and Rules of Operation

Unit 7: **Fractions**
Addition, Subtraction, Multiplication and Division of Fractions

Unit 8: **Mixed Numerals**
Working with expressions that are a combination of fractions and whole numbers

Unit 9: **Decimal**
Operation on decimals

Unit 10: **Mathematical Expressions**
Understanding Expression and Equations

Unit 11: **Test 1** – *(Focused on concepts in unit 2 – unit 10)*

Unit 12: **Rounding and Estimates**
Rounding & Estimating

Unit 13: **Exponents and Scientific Notation**
Working with Exponents and Scientific Notations

Unit 14:	**Additive and Multiplicative Property**	
	Methods of solving Linear Equations with one variable	

Unit 14:   **Additive and Multiplicative Property**
Methods of solving Linear Equations with one variable

Unit 15:   **Linear Inequalities**
Working with Equations vs. Inequalities

Unit 16:   **Linear Equations in One Variable**
Working with Equations with one unknown

Unit 17:   **An Introduction to Problem Solving**
Solving word problems

Unit 18:   **Formulas and Problem Solving**
Working with Formulas

Unit 19:   **Test 2** – *(Focused on concepts in unit 12 – unit 18)*

Unit 20:   **Geometry**
Basic Geometrical shapes

Unit 21:   **Ratio, Rate and Proportion**
Working with Ratio, Rate and Proportion

Unit 22:   **Percentage and Applications of Percent**
Working with Percentages

Unit 23:   **Interest**
Simple and Compound Interests

Unit 24:   **Graphing Linear Equations**
Fundamentals of drawing Graphs

Unit 25:   **Test 3** – *(Focused on concepts in unit 20 – unit 24)*

Unit 26:   **Introduction to Polynomials**
Understanding the *Fundamentals of Polynomials*

Unit 27:   **Addition and Subtraction of Polynomials**
Add and Subtract Polynomials

Unit 28:   **Multiplication of Polynomials**
Distributive, Long Multiplication and FOIL Methods

Unit 29:   **Special Products**
Perfect Square and Difference of Squares

Unit 30:	**Division of Polynomials**
Dividing by Monomials and Binomials
Unit 31:	**Test 4** – *(Focused on concepts in unit 26 – unit 30)*
Unit 32:	**Factoring**
Introduction to Factoring
Unit 33:	**Greatest Common Factor**
Factoring by finding the GCF
Unit 34:	**Grouping**
Factor by Grouping
Unit 35:	**Trail & Error**
Factor by Trial & Error
Unit 36:	**AC - Method**
AC-Method of Factoring
Unit 37:	**Factoring Strategies**
General Factoring Strategies
Unit 38:	**Zero Property**
Method of solving Quadratic Equations
Unit 39:	**Square Root & Completing the Square**
Other method of solving Quadratic Equations
Unit 40:	**The Quadratic Formula**
Application of the Quadratic Formula
Unit 41:	**Test 5** – *(Focused on concepts in units 32– unit 40)*

Concept Application - *(Activities to demonstrate knowledge)*

Appendix

Solution and Answers

Index

ALGEBRA MADE EASY UNIT 1
How to Succeed- Get an attitude

Learning Objective
After completing this section, you should be able to:

1. Develop a plan on how to approach your math education.

Introduction:

Get an attitude:
That is right; believe it or not your ability to succeed in math depends a lot on your attitude toward math and how you apply yourself. If you tell yourself that you are not good at math then you have set the precedence to fail. Why? You will have a mind block and will retain little or nothing that you have been taught. If you tell yourself that you can do it, you are going to look for opportunity to improve yourself and you will apply yourself.

Start off by cleaning out your thought closet when it comes to math.

In mathematics the more that you practice the better you get.

Hopefully by the end of these units you would have gotten some practice and see an improvement in your math skills.

Getting Started:

The average person always asks the questions **"why do I have to learn algebra"**. I want to challenge you to not look at algebra as just about addition and multiplication. Learning algebra is learning problem solving techniques; it is about your ability to analyze information, draw conclusion and then take action. You will be picking up on that as you solve word problems.

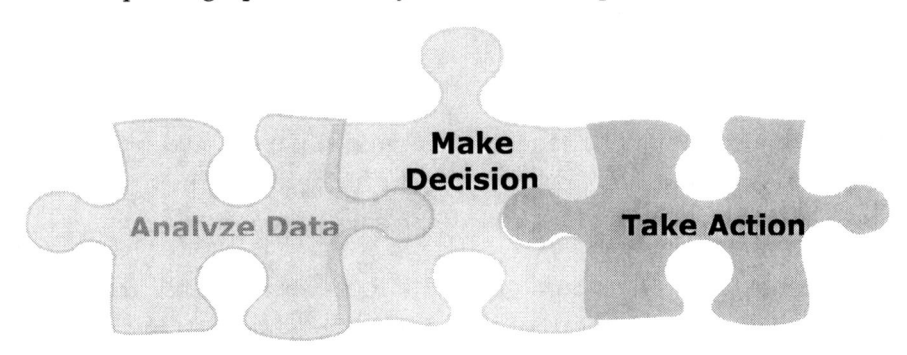

Analyze Data → **Make Decision** → **Take Action**

Let's say that you are planning to take a family vacation, how would you go about doing it?

- You would decide how much money to allocate for the vacation
- Then you would decide where to go
- Then you would decide how to get there
- Then you would decide where to stay, etc.

ALGEBRA MADE EASY – A Practical Approach to Algebra

By the time you got to the final decision you would have taken a lot of things into consideration. In doing so you were analyzing information and drawing conclusions or making decisions.

That is the essence of what you are doing in algebra, you are analyzing information, making decisions and taking an action. Or suppose that you had $10 and you wanted to buy lunch. Your sandwich + your drink + chips (or fries) + tax must be less than or equal to the amount of money that you have, agreed? Do you see the use of algebra anywhere there?

Do not focus so much on the problems that you are doing but more on the skill set that you're gaining and the discipline that you have developed as a result of working on the problems.

- First you consider what needs to be done
- Then you review the various choices
- Finally a decision is made.

Get the "Yes I CAN Attitude:

If you are living and breathing you are using algebra so tell yourself that you can do it. It is like the air that you breathe; you cannot get away from it.

Practice, Practice, Practice:

Math is an application subject therefore you are not going to grasp the concept by looking at someone else doing the problems. You have to do it for yourself, remember this philosophy *"the more that you practice the better you get."*

Develop a study plan that includes time set aside for reading, practice and assignments. Researchers say that after seven times something becomes a habit, so you should plan to practice at least seven (7) problems on each concept. You should plan to spend a few hours each week that you are registered for class working on math.

Show up and Get Help:

More than likely if you knew the material already you would have tested out of the class. So if you sign up for the class; go to class and don't be afraid to ask for help. Instructors usually like students to ask for help because it is an indication that you are doing some work outside of class.

In addition to this material, take advantage of all the tools and services that your institution has available. And don't forget the most obvious one, which is to read the text book.

Don't Give UP:

If at first you don't understand speak up and ask for clarification. Never let the class proceed if you do not understand a concept. If you do, you are more than likely going to be lost from that point forward. Keep in mind that each concept is the building block for the next so if you miss a concept that is a good chance that you will also missed the one after that.

Apply Yourself:

All math concepts are geared toward answering a question, so whenever you learn a concept try to apply it outside of the classroom that week. You will be amazed how that will help you retain and understand a concept.

Learn the Basics:

Look at algebra as building on a foundation four pillars.

ADDITION   SUBTRACTION   MULTIPLICATION   DIVISION

Everything that you do will involve a combination or one or more of those operations. Every time that you learn a new concept you will be learning how to perform these four operations on that concept.

Do the Research:

The first step to solve any problem correctly is to first understand what you have been asked to do. If you come across a terminology that you do not know, stop and look it up. If you need a formula and it was not given, stop and look it up.

Use Your Tools: – *(The toolbox Approach)*

Look at your learning as a tool box and that each concept that you learn is another tool that is being applied to your **toolbox**. Whenever you get a problem to solve you should look at the problem and then decide which tool you have that can be apply to solve that problem. Keep in mind that your tools can come from sources outside you current class, such as another class, a friend, or life experience. Also keep in mind that you might need to apply more than one tool at different points in order to solve a problem.

Apply reasoning and logic when solving word problems and note that the theory tells you the process (that is, how to do it) and logic and reasoning help you determine what to do.

ALGEBRA MADE EASY UNIT 2
Real Numbers

More than likely when you were a toddler just after you learned to say "No", "Yes", "Mommy" and or "Daddy", you learned to say "One, Two, Three". What you were doing is learning to count.
The number system is made up of counting numbers.

```
0    1    2    3    4   5   6   7   8   9
10   11   12   13   14  15  16  17  ... 99
100  101  102  103  104 ...
```

These numbers are called **Whole Numbers.**

Look closely and you will notice that all numbers consists of the first ten digits arranged differently. Each arrangement produces a different number that has a unique value.

Since numbers have similar digits we have to determine a way to differentiate the various numbers. To do that, mathematicians came up with a value chart that determines the value of the digit depending on where it appears in the number.

Place Value Chart

Periods →

Trillions			Billions			Millions			Thousands			Ones		
		1	0	0	1	2	1	5	4	1	2	6	2	3
Hundreds	Tens	Ones	Hundreds	Tens	Ones	Hundreds	Tens	Ones	Hundreds	Tens	Ones	Hundreds	Tens	Ones

1 Trillion   1 Billion   215 Millions   412 Thousands   623 Ones

For example, in the number 623 since there are only three digits we know that we are dealing with a value in the hundreds. Now to determine the exact value of the number you start with the last digit and that is of value Ones, the next digit will be Tens and the third digit will be Hundreds.

Therefore the number **623** is **Six Hundred, Two Tens and Three Ones**

Because of the way we speak we would simply say **Six Hundred and Twenty Three.**

Note also that you can use this process to determine the values of single digits in a number. For example what is the value of the **2** in **4237**?

Solution: The 2 is equivalent to **Two Hundred.**

The mathematical term for this is *Expanded Notation of Numbers*. That is simply writing out the number in words that represents the value of each digit.

Example: **Writing out Numbers**
Write expanded notation for 5280.

Solution
5280 = **Five thousands + Two hundreds + Eight Tens + Zero Ones**

More than likely you have been using this concept but might not have considered it to be math. When you first learned it you just did it because you were told that is what should be done to achieve your goal.

There is also a concept known as *Standard Notation* which is simply the opposite of expanded notation.

Let's look at an example

Three Hundred and Forty Eight written in expanded notation is 300 + 40 + 8

Note that

- The 3 is in the hundred position that is the reason why it is 300,
- The 4 is in the ten positions that is the reason why it is represented as 40 and
- The 8 is in the ones position that is the reason why it is represented by 8

Now when you have the expanded notation and you want to write it back as one number it becomes *standard notation*. In our example above Three Hundred and Forty Eight becomes 348.

You might be asking the question why I need to learn the difference. Recall earlier I said that more than likely have been using this concept and not realize it? Let's look at a use of expanded and standard notations are used.

Expanded Notation
Application Example
Let's say that you were writing a check for $1386
- How would you write the amount on the check?

Solution

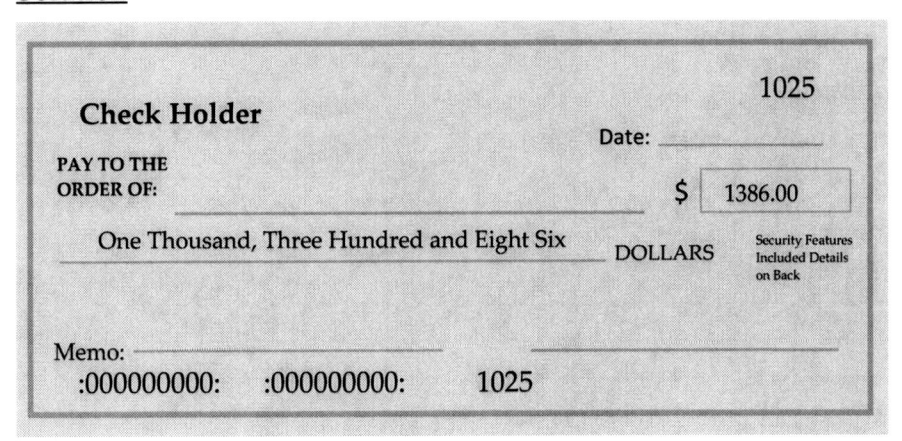

```
                                                          1025
  Check Holder
                                    Date: _____
  PAY TO THE
  ORDER OF: _____  $  1386.00

  ___One Thousand, Three Hundred and Eight Six___  DOLLARS   Security Features
                                                             Included Details
                                                             on Back

  Memo: _____  _____
  :000000000:   :000000000:   1025
```

Note that amount on the line is written in *expanded notation* and the amount in the box in the upper right hand corner is written in *standard notation*.

Does any of this look familiar?

If you have ever written a check it should.

Real Number Exercise

1. Write the following in standard notation.
   One Million and sixty five dollars

2. Write the following in expanded notation.
   144

3. Think of two other examples like the one above where you have used standard notations.
4. Think of two other examples like the one above where you have used expanded notations.

Concept Application

1) **Purchase:** You are ordering party favors for a 10 year old birthday party. Each item cost $3.25 and you are expecting 30 children to be in attendance. Fill in the order form from HAL Specialty Supplies.

Order Form

Ship To:

Quantity	Description	Unit Price	Total Price
		Total	$

Solution at the end of this unit.

Solution to Concept Application

Quantity	Description	Unit Price	Total Price
30	Children Party Favors	$3.25	$97.50
		Total	$97.50

ALGEBRA MADE EASY UNIT 3
The Number System

In mathematics numbers are put into different categories to help us understand and differentiate between them. In this unit we are going to look at the different categories that define numbers.

A **set** is a collection of objects which is denoted by being included within curly brackets. In this material we will consider sets of numbers. For example, the set containing the numbers 0, 2, and 5 is written as {0, 2, 5}. Sets that are part of other sets are called **subsets**. For example the set of even numbers in 0, 2, and 5 is written as {2}. Therefore {2} is a subset of {0, 2, 5}.

Types of numbers

- Natural numbers: example {1, 2, 3, 4, 5, . . .}
    Natural numbers are the ordinary counting numbers 1, 2, 3, etc.
- Whole numbers: example {0, 1, 2, 3, 4, 5, . . .}
    Whole numbers is the set of all natural numbers plus 0.
- Integers: example {. . . , -3, -2, -1, 0, 1, 2, 3, . . .}
    An **integer** is the set of all positive and negative whole numbers.
- Rational numbers defined by a/b, where $b \neq 0$
    Rational number is any number that <u>can</u> be expressed as the quotient a/b of two integers, with the denominator b not equal to zero.
- Irrational numbers e.g. $\sqrt{2}, \sqrt{5}, \varepsilon$, etc.
    $\sqrt{2} = 1.4142...$ $\sqrt{5} = 2.23606...$ $\varepsilon = 2.7142...$
    Irrational number is any real number which <u>cannot</u> be expressed as the quotient of integers, that is like a fraction a/b.
- Real numbers are numbers which can be represented by points on a number line.
    A **real number** is a value that represents a quantity.

See the chart below for examples of each category of numbers.

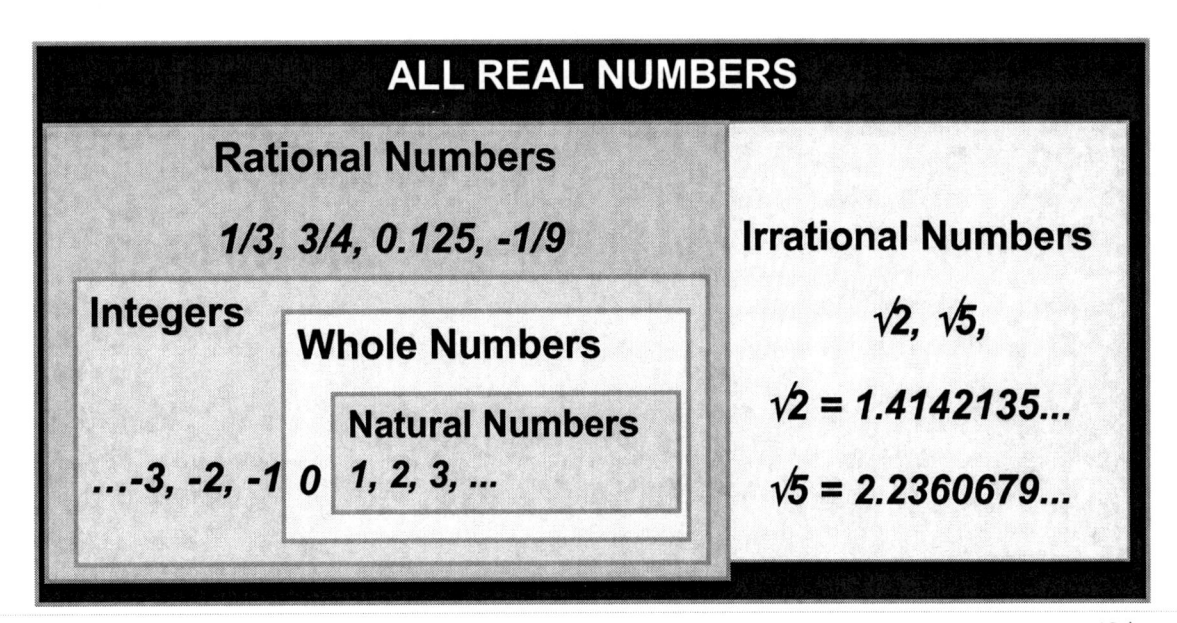

ALL REAL NUMBERS

Rational Numbers

1/3, 3/4, 0.125, -1/9

Integers

...-3, -2, -1

Whole Numbers

0

Natural Numbers

1, 2, 3, ...

Irrational Numbers

$\sqrt{2}, \sqrt{5},$

$\sqrt{2} = 1.4142135...$

$\sqrt{5} = 2.2360679...$

ALGEBRA MADE EASY – A Practical Approach to Algebra

Note that some of categories of numbers are subset of another category. For example natural numbers are a subset of whole numbers. *See if you can identify any other subsets.*

Number System Exercise
1. Are all Integers Natural Numbers?
2. Are all Integers Rational Numbers?
3. Is $\sqrt{9}$ a natural number?
4. Is $\sqrt{10}$ a rational or an irrational number?
5. Are all natural numbers integers?
6. Are all Whole numbers real numbers?
7. Are all Rational numbers natural numbers?
8. Classify the follow as either Natural Numbers, Whole, Numbers, Integer, Rational Numbers, Irrational Number or Real Numbers.
   5, ½, $\sqrt{16}$, $\sqrt{11}$, 3/7, -27, 0

Keep in mind that some numbers may fall in more than one category

Concept Application
1) ***Salary***: Is the amount of earnings on your pay check represented by a Natural number or an Integer?
2) ***Finance***: Is the balance owed on your credit card an example of a Natural number or an Integer?

Solutions at the end of this unit.

Solutions to Concept Application
1) *Natural number, your wages should not be negative*
2) *An Integer, the balance on the credit card can be negative*

ALGEBRA MADE EASY UNIT 4
Operation Of Real Numbers

Math as a Language
As with any language, there are rules of syntax and grammar. It is essential to know these rules so that the receiver and the sender can be in sync with each other. You should not try to prove those rules you should just accept and use them and believe that by applying those rules correctly you will arrive at the correct solution.

In this material you will be presented with some information that will not be proven however you will need to accept and use them. Every time that you come across one of those think of it as a gift.

Algebraic Syntax (Symbols)
There are some mathematical syntax that you will need to know in order to be able to understand mathematical expressions. Here are a few of those syntaxes to keep in mind.

> = This sign reads "equal to"
> ≠ This sign reads "not equal to"
> < This sign reads "less than"
> > This sign reads "greater than"
> ≤ This sign reads "less than or equal to"
> ≥ This sign reads "greater than or equal to"

How these syntaxes were developed is beyond the scope of this material.

There are four basic fundamental mathematic operations; earlier they were referred to as the four pillars of algebra.

Addition
The first one that we are going to look at is **Addition**.
In English we use conjunctions like "**AND**" to join thoughts and ideas together.
   For example Jack and Jill

In Math we use the operation "**Addition**" to join thoughts together. The symbol used to represent addition is (+). Some other terminologies that also mean addition are:
- Plus
- Sum

For example Jack + Jill
Now that we know that Addition is the process of putting things together let's look at an example using addition.

Maisy has three mugs and she purchased two more mugs, how much mugs does Maisy now have?

   3 mugs   +   2 mugs   Combined we have 5 mugs

As you see there were 3 mugs and when combined with two more mugs she got a total of 5 mugs.

Addition Example1:
Write an addition sentence that corresponds to this situation.

Rhea has 3 DVD's and Mom purchases 4 more for her. How many DVD's does Rhea have in all?

Solution

An addition sentence that corresponds is 3 + 4 for a total of 7.
Can also be written as 3 + 4 = 7

Addition Example2
Travel: Colieman drives 25 miles from Home to I-275 and another 10 miles from there to get to work each day. How many miles does Colieman drive to work each day?

Solution

25 mi + 10 mi for a total of 35 miles to work each day
Can also be written as 25 mi + 10 mi = 35 mi

Now let's expand that knowledge to add whole numbers.

The process works the same irrespective of the number that you are working with (whole number, fraction, and decimal). For now we will focus on whole numbers. Once you grasp the concept with whole numbers it will be easy to apply it to other type numbers.

Whole Number Addition *Example 1*: Add 6878 to 995

Solution

The best way to add numbers is to line them up in columns so that the corresponding values appears in a column

```
  6 8 7 8
+   9 9 5     (Remember the = sign?)
  7 8 7 3
```

To complete the addition process, combine the columns.

Keep in mind that you cannot have any more than 9 ONES therefore anything above that is converted to TENS. Similarly, you cannot have more than 9 TENS therefore anything above that is converted to HUNDREADS. Since you cannot have more than 9 HUNDREADS anything above that is converted to HOUSANDS. And that continues on until you have accounted for all the columns.

Note that the biggest number that can be in any of the columns is 9.

Whole Number Addition *Example 2*: Add 4597 to 3682

Solution

```
  4 5 9 7
+ 3 6 8 2
  8 2 7 9
```

Whole Numbers Addition Exercise

Do the following without using a calculator.
1. Add 565 to 84
2. Add 106 to 94

Subtraction

The second operation that we will look at is **Subtraction**.

In English we use phrase like "**TAKE AWAY**" to separate things.

> For example take the book off the table

In Math we take from things together by **Subtracting**. The symbol used is (-). Some other terminologies that also mean subtraction are:

- Minus
- From

For example **table - Book**

As you can see Subtraction is the process of separating. Now let us look at an example.

Subtraction Example 1

In his book bag Khal has 8 pens. He gave his friend 3 of the pens. How many pens does Khal have remaining?

Solution

There were **8** to start with and he *gave away* **3** therefore he has **5** remaining.

Whole Number Subtraction *Example 1*: Subtract 281 from 493 *(interpreted as 493 - 281)*

Solution   Place the numbers in columns so that the like numbers line up

```
  4 9 3
- 2 8 1
  2 1 2
```

Once the numbers are lined up in columns, subtract the columns.

Whole Number Subtraction *Example 2*: 538 - 261

<u>Solution</u>   Place the numbers in columns so that the like numbers line up

```
   4 13
   5̶ 3̶ 8
 - 2 6 1
   2 7 7
```

Notice that you can take 1 from 8 quite easily. Now to take 6 from 3, since 6 is bigger than 3, you have to go over to the next column and borrow 1. Note the column that you are in and the actual value of that 1. The 1 that was borrowed from the 5 when placed in the second column became 10. *10 + 3 = 13* and then you can subtract 6 from 13 to get 7. Keep in mind that when you borrowed 1 the 5 became 4.

Subtraction Example 3

Travel: To get to work Colieman can take one of two routes. Route A will take 45 minutes and route B will take 58 minutes. How much time will Colieman save if he takes route A to work?

<u>Solution</u>

Route B - Route A   = Savings
   58   -   45   = 13 minutes

Subtraction Example 4

Purchase: Kim wants to buy her graduation ring. The ring cost $599 and she has $200. How much more money does Kim needs.

<u>Solution</u>

To find the answer, we subtract the amount of money that she has form the cost.
599 – 200 = 300

Kim needs $300 more to be able to purchase the ring.

<u>Whole Numbers Subtraction Exercise</u>
Do the following without using a calculator.
1. Subtract 84 from 500
2. Subtract 94 from 250

Multiplication
The third operation that we will look at is **Multiplication**.

Multiplication is simply repeated addition. When dealing with small numbers it might be sufficient to just add.

Example

Khal has some pennies that he stacked in groups of 3s. If he had 2 groups of those stacks of pennies, how many pennies does he have total?

           Group 1   **Group 2**

3 + 3 = 6

That can also be represented as 3 x 2 = 6 meaning 2 groups of 3 pennies the total is 6.

When working with larger numbers it is simplest to multiply. For example 10 0 x 2 = 200.

In Math the symbol (**x**) is used to represent **Multiplication**. Some other terminologies that also mean multiplication are:

- Times
- By
- Product
- Of

Multiplication Example 1

    3   x   2 = 6

The numbers that are multiplied are called *factors* and the result is called the *product*.

Multiplication Example 2: 24 x 2

Solution

```
  2 4
x   2
─────
  3 8
```

Long Multiplication

To combine numbers where the multiplier is greater than 9 we use a process called **long multiplication**. Let's look at an example.

Long Multiplication Example 1:

```
    7 4 6
x     6 2
```

Solution
To arrive at the answer we will first multiple 746 by 2 and then multiply it by 60 and add the results.

```
        7 4 6
  x      6 2
      1 4 9 2   ← Multiplying first by 2
  + 4 4 7 6 0   ← Multiply next by 60
    4 6,2 5 2   ← Add the results
```

Note to multiply by a number that is of value 10 you write a 0 first and then multiply by the number. (*Refer to the value chart under whole numbers*)

> **Multiplication Tips**
>
> Here are a few tips to keep in mind when multiplying.
>
> If *a* is used to represent a randomly selected number, then
> - **Zero times any number is always Zero.**
> $0 * a = 0$
>   *Example: It makes no sense to ask how many ways zero can be combined together.*
>
> - **One times any number is the number itself**
> $1 * a = a$
>   *Example: A single item can only be arranged into a group of 1*

Whole Numbers Multiplication Exercise

Do the following without using a calculator.
1. Multiply 222 by 16
2. Multiply 19 by 35
3. 68 x 76
4. 56 x 1
5. 634 x 0

Division

The fourth and final mathematical operation that we will look at is **Division**.

Division is simply repeated subtraction.

When dealing with small numbers it might be sufficient to just subtract. However, when dealing with large numbers we need to find a less cumbersome and time consuming process of deriving the solution.

Let's look at this example

> How many stacks of 5 books can you get from the 20 books in the original stack?

Original stack

4 Stocks of 5 books

Solution

We can make stacks of books 4 high until all the books in the original pile have been used up.

Since there are 4 sets of 5 books each, we get that 20 ÷ 5 = 4

> **The number which is reduced is called the *Dividend*, the number used to do the reduction is called the *Divisor* and the result is called the *Quotient*.**

In Math the symbol (÷) is used to represent **Division**. Some other terminologies that also mean multiplication are:
- Divide
- Quotient

If you have ever played a card game then you have used the concept of division. When the deck of cards is being distributed among the players you are simple dividing the 52 cards among the total number of players.

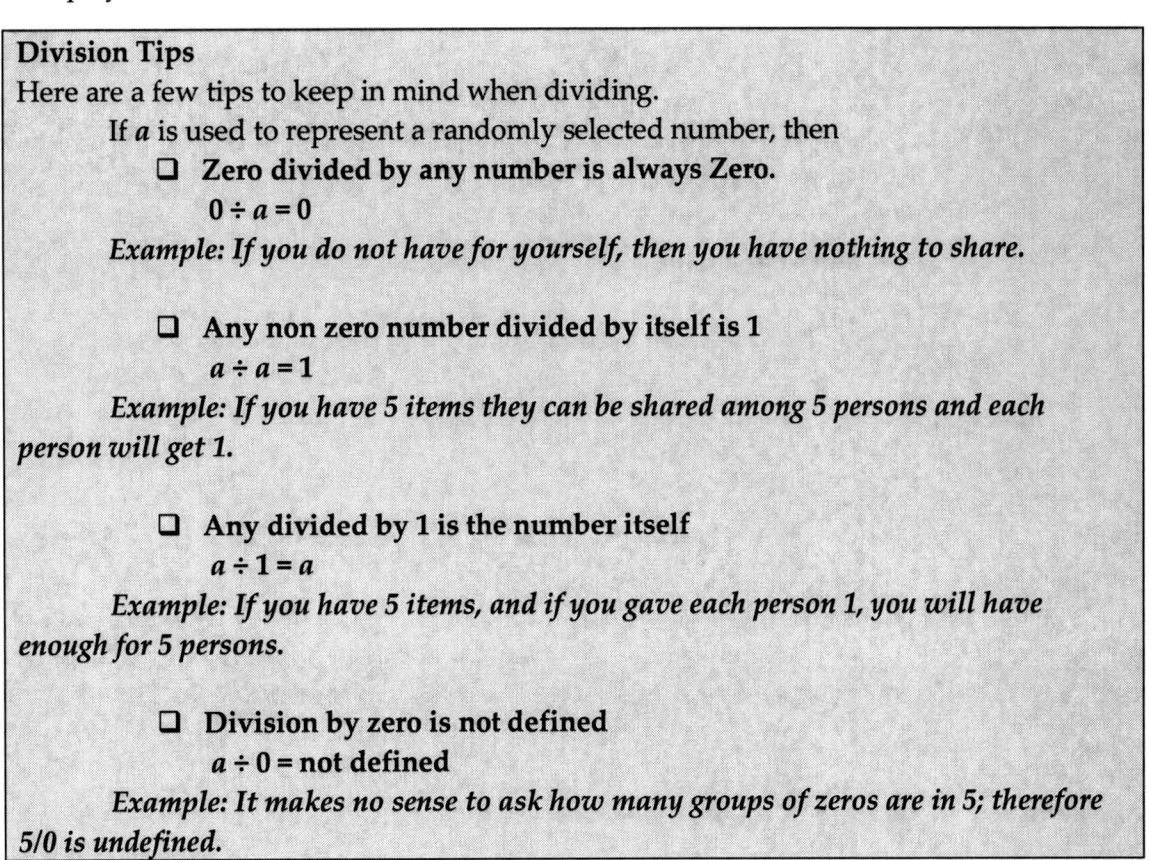

> **Division Tips**
> Here are a few tips to keep in mind when dividing.
> If a is used to represent a randomly selected number, then
> - ❑ **Zero divided by any number is always Zero.**
> $0 \div a = 0$
>   *Example: If you do not have for yourself, then you have nothing to share.*
>
> - ❑ **Any non zero number divided by itself is 1**
> $a \div a = 1$
>   *Example: If you have 5 items they can be shared among 5 persons and each person will get 1.*
>
> - ❑ **Any divided by 1 is the number itself**
> $a \div 1 = a$
>   *Example: If you have 5 items, and if you gave each person 1, you will have enough for 5 persons.*
>
> - ❑ **Division by zero is not defined**
> $a \div 0 =$ not defined
>   *Example: It makes no sense to ask how many groups of zeros are in 5; therefore 5/0 is undefined.*

Long Division

To separate a number that does not divide evenly into groups we go through a process called long division.

Example: 100 divided by 3

Solution

```
      33
   3)100      Start by saying 3 divided by 1; I can't. Then add the next digit to 1 to get 10 (Steps 1 & 2)
    -9        10 divided 3; the result is 3 (Step 3)
     10       3 times 3 = 9, so minus 9 from 10. Bring down the other 0 and that another 10 (Steps 4 & 5)
     -9       3 into 10 goes 3 times (Step 6)
      1       3 times 3 = 9, so minus 9 from 10. This leaves a remainder of 1 (Steps 7 & 8)
```

The solution is 33 with remainder 1

Steps
1. You may say 3 divided by 1; I can't,
2. So add the next digit to 1 to get 10
3. Then say 10 divided 3; the result is 3 (that is 10 can be divided into 3 groups of 3's)
4. Then 3 times 3 = 9, so minus 9 from 10 (that is 10 can be divided into 3 groups of 3's and there is 1 remaining)
5. Bring down the other 0 and that makes another 10
6. Again 3 goes into 10 goes 3 times (see explanation for step 3)
7. Again 3 times 3 = 9, so minus 9 from 10 (see explanation for step 4)
8. This leaves a remainder of 1

(Use a similar process for other numbers that you will divide)

Whole Numbers Division Exercise

Do the following without using a calculator.
1. Divide 21 by 4
2. 35 ÷ 5
3. Divide 631 by 15
4. 5 ÷ 0
5. 0 ÷ 35

Solutions to Concept Application
1) 150/2 = 70 remainder 10. Each child will get $70 and Maisy will have $10 remaining.
2) 35 * 4 = 140, Rhea will be paid $140 at the end of the week.

Concept Application

1) *Entertainment*: Maisy has two daughters and she is sending them to the local fair. She has $150 how much will each child receive if she gives them the same amount and how much will she have remaining?
2) *Salary*: Rhea babysat for 4 hours this week. She earns a rate of $35 per hour, how much will she be paid at the end of the week?

Solutions at the side.

ALGEBRA MADE EASY UNIT 5
Negative Numbers

To understand numbers we use the number line and look at where the numbers appear on the number line. Integers consist of the whole numbers and their opposites with zero being the dividing point in the center.

Numbers that appear to the left of zero on the number line is the exact opposite of the numbers in the same position to the right of the number line. *See figure 1.*

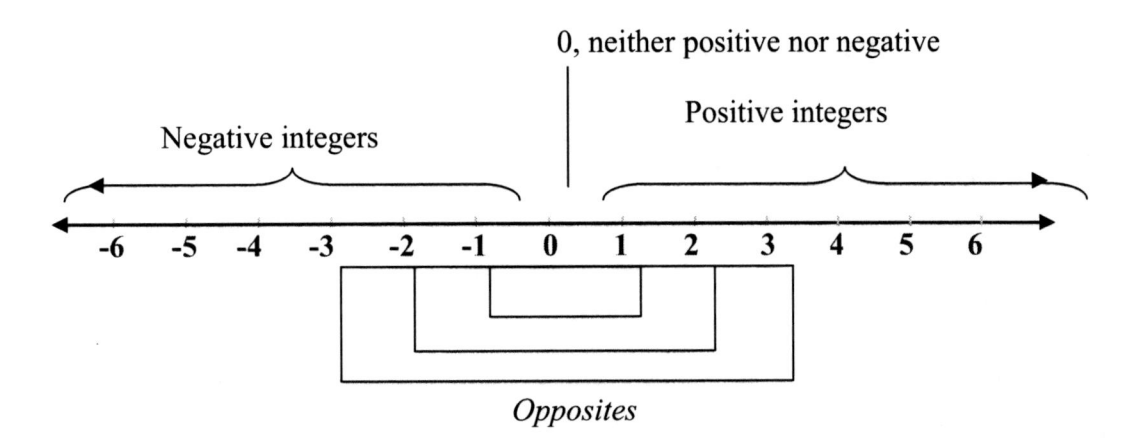

Figure 1

The numbers to the left of the 0 are called *negative numbers*. Some common uses for negative numbers are:

Money: Example: debits, loans, money spent, withdrawals
Temperature: Example 20 degrees below 0 degrees, -20^0
Evaluation: Example 100 ft below sea level, -100ft

Note that while zero is the dividing point between negative and positive numbers; zero itself is neither positive nor negative. It has no sign.

Negative numbers are also called the *opposite* of a number. So if the number that you are looking for is represented by x then the opposite or negative of x is written $-x$.

To find the negative or opposite of a number you simply change the sign. That is, consider that you are looking in a mirror and the opposite is looking back at you. For example the opposite of 1 is -1. *See figure 1.*

(Note: To determine whether or not you are talking about negative x (-x) or minus x (-x) will be dependent on the context in which the information is used). This is similar to what you do in English.

Example 1
Maisy has a credit card balance of $253; write an integer to represent Maisy's balance.

Solution
Since Maisy owes the money, we can write the amount as **-$253**.

Example 2
Maisy spent $253 on her credit card and she deposited $300 in her bank account. Write integers to represent Maisy's activities.

Solution
Since Maisy spent the $253 that is represented by **-$253**.
Since she deposited $300 that is represented by **$300**.

Example 3
The Dow Jones lost 300 points today. Write an integer to represent the loss.

Solution
Since the Dow Jones went down that is represented by **-300**.

Adding Negative numbers

To understand the addition of negative you need to consider where you started and where you end up relative to zero on the number line. To perform the addition of two integers for example $a + b$, on the number line we start at a, and then move to b in the direction of the sign stated. The result is going to be the new location in relationship to 0.

> **Steps to perform addition**
> a) If b is positive, we move to the right.
> b) If b is negative, we move to the left.
> c) If b is 0, we stay at a.

Negative Addition Example 1:
Add: $4 + (-6)$

Solution

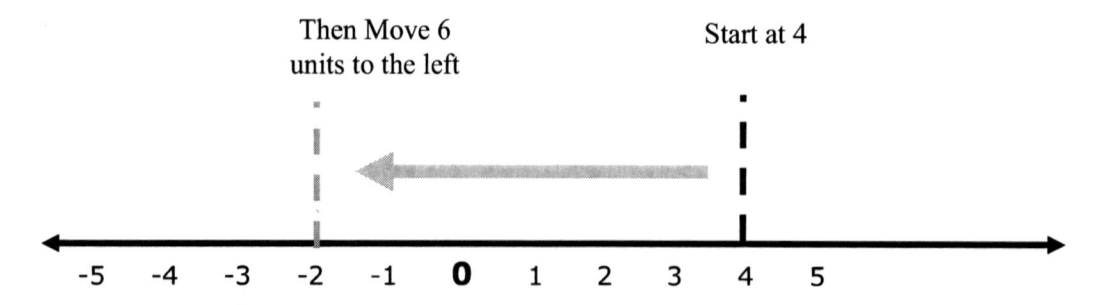

```
        Then Move 6              Start at 4
        units to the left
           ←────────────────────
   ─┼────┼────┼────┼────┼────┼────┼────┼────┼────┼────→
   -5   -4   -3   -2   -1   0    1    2    3    4    5
```

The last position is 2 to the left of 0.
The result of $4 + -6 = $ **-2**

Negative Addition Example 2:
Add: −3 + 5
Solution

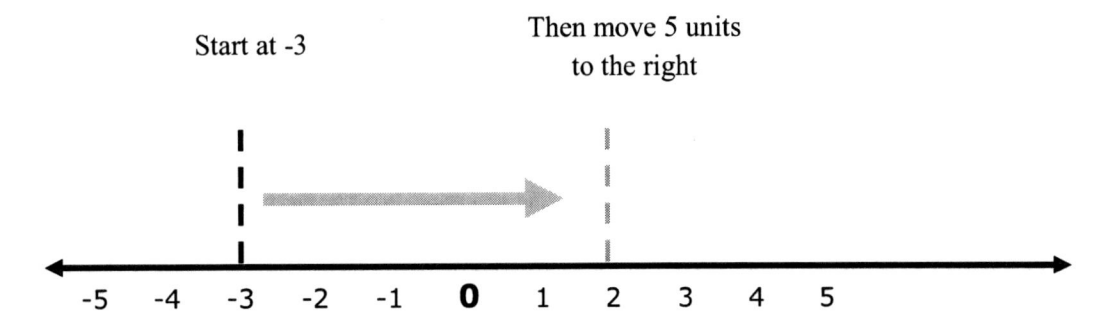

```
        Start at -3              Then move 5 units
                                   to the right
```

<--|----|----|----|----|----|----|----|----|----|----|-->
   -5   -4   -3   -2   -1   0   1   2   3   4   5

The last position is 2 to the right of 0.
The result of −3 + 5 = **2**

Note that adding negative numbers is similar to subtraction.

Negative Addition Example 3:
Serma has a loan balance of $150 she earned $125 this week. She also has to gas card bill of $40. What is Serma's financial standing at the end of the week?

Solution
Serma's Income $125
Serma's Debt   -$150 & -$40

To find out how much she has remaining at the end of the week, we add all the amounts
$125 + -$150 + -$40 = -$65

At the end of the week Serma is still $65 in debt.

Negative Numbers Exercise
Write an integer to represent the following;
1) A balance of $687.63 on a credit card
2) A credit of $23.46 to an account
3) 10 degrees below zero
4) 150 feet below sea level
5) 300 feet about the ground

Concept Application
1) *Bill Payment:* Dominique has a phone bill in the amount of $123.97 and she got paid $800 at the end of the week. How much does Dominique have remaining after paying the phone bill?
Solution at the end of this unit.

Solutions to Concept Application
1) $800 − 123.97 = $676.03

ALGEBRA MADE EASY UNIT 6
Properties Of Real Number

As with everything else there are certain standards that are adopted in algebra to ensure that regardless of who does the calculations or where the calculations are done the result will be the same. In this unit we will look at the order of operations, the rules of operation as well as the properties of real numbers sometimes referred to as the laws of algebra.

Order of Operations
There is a certain order in which operations must be carried out in order to obtain the correct results.

Rules involved in order of operations are as follows:
1. Perform operations inside grouping symbols first
2. Simplify exponential expressions next
3. Do multiplication or division as they occur Left to Right
4. Finally do addition and subtraction as they occur Left to Right

Note that we did not prove these rules; they are standards that we must abide by.

These rules can be easily remembered by the acronym:
P arentheses
E xponents
M ultiplication
D ivision
A ddition
S ubtraction

(You might even heard it referred to as Please Excuse My Dear Aunt Sally)

Properties of Real Numbers
In addition to the order of operations, there are also some properties that we need to abide by. Those properties are discussed in this next section.

Commutative Property
The commutative property states that changing the order of a statement, does not change the end result.

For example the price of a slice of pizza and drink is the same as the price of the drink and the slice of pizza. *Example: 2 + 5 is the same as 5 + 2; that is 7 = 7.*

If you wanted to purchase 2 drinks the price would be the same if you purchased drink1 then drink2 or drink2 then drink1. *Example: 2*5 is the same as 5*2; that is 10 = 10.*

Addition	$A + B = B + A$
Multiplication	$AB = BA$

Note that the *Commutative Property* only applies to addition and multiplication.

Associative Property

The associative properties states that you can re-group members without changing the result.

For example if you purchase fries, a hamburger, and then a Coke. The result will be the same as if you purchase the coke and the hamburger and then the fires.

Addition Example: 2 + (3 + 4) is the same as (2 + 3) + 4, that is 2 + (7) = (5) + 4 the result is 9 = 9.
Multiplication Example: 2*(3*4) is the same as (2*3)*4, that is 2*(12) = (6)*4 the result is 24 = 24.

    Addition $(a + b) + c = a + (b + c)$
    Multiplication $(ab)c = a(bc)$

> **Note that like the commutative property the *Associative Property* only applies to addition and multiplication.**

Distributive Property

The Distributive property let's you multiply a sum by multiplying each term separately and then add the products.

    For example, let's say you have to quickly multiply: 3 x 23
                  (3 x 20) + (3 x 3)
                  60 + 9
                  69

If you were doing this in your head without a calculator you could quickly compute the answer of 3x20 (60) then add (3x3) 9 to give 69.

For any real number
                        $a(b + c) = ab + ac$
         and $a(b - c) = ab - ac$

> **In algebra the *Distributive Property* is used mainly to help you get rid of parentheses.**

In math when you are asked **evaluate** something you are simply being asked to calculate the answer. For example, evaluate the following expression. $3(2x - 1) - 2(2x - 3)$ for $x = 2$ is asking you to find a numerical value for the expression for the given value of $x = 2$.

Solution:

To find the value you would replace x by 2 and then carry out the indicated operation. $3(2x - 1) - 2(2x - 3) = (3)(2•2 - 1) - 2(2•2 - 3) = 3(4 - 1) - 2(4 - 3) = 3(3) - 2(1) = 9 - 2 = 7$

However, to **simplify** an expression is to break the expression down into its simplest form. Example 10/12 can be broken down to 5/6. Here you find a number that is common to both the numerator and the denominator and factor it out. In the example 2 can divide both 10 and 12 evenly. 10 = 2•5 and 12 = 2•6. So $\frac{10}{12} = \frac{2•5}{2•6} = \frac{2}{2} • \frac{5}{6} = \frac{5}{6}$ since 2/2 = 1.

$4x + 2y - x = 3x + 2y$. Here you identify the things that are alike and combine them using the appropriate operation. *(This will be discussed in details later)*

Properties of Real Number Exercise
Simplify the following;
1. $3 + 4^2 - 5$
2. $21/7 + 4 - 3 \cdot 2$
3. $2(5)^2 - 10) + 4 \cdot 3 \div 2$
4. $21 \div 3 + 7$
5. $3 - 2 + 35 \div 7$

Absolute Value

The *Absolute Value* of a number is the distance of a number from zero; that is the positive value of a number.

Use your imagination for the next few minutes as we play a simple game of blind-mans-buff. Let's say that you were blindfolded and put into a room and were told that there is a sandwich in the room at some point unknown to you. The only information that you are given is that you have to take 2 steps from where you are to get to the sandwich.

First you might take two steps to the right to see if the sandwich is there, what distance did you travel? **Two steps;** on *the number line this would be represented as +2.*

If you did not find the sandwich there the next logical thing to do is to return to the original spot and take two steps to the left this time. Again, what distance did you travel in the left direction? **Two steps,** on *the number line this would be represented as -2.*

If someone asked you what distance you traveled to find the sandwich you would have said 2 steps to the left, notice that you will not say -2 steps.

If you got or gave directions to anyone you have been using the concept of absolute value. 2 miles east is the same as saying 2 miles to the right or +2 miles and 2 miles west is the same as saying 2 miles to the left or -2 miles.

Rules Of Operation
Not to be confused with the *Order of Operation* is the *Rules of Operation*. The process of working with real numbers is the same irrespective of what the form the numbers are in. The process is stated as rules for each type of operation and then demonstrated.

Rules for Multiplication of Real Numbers
1. Multiply the absolute values, if the signs are the same the result is positive
2. Multiply the absolute values, if the signs are different the result is negative

Multiplication Examples
1. $2 * 3 = 6$ *Both numbers are positive*

	-2 * -3 = 6	*Both numbers are negative*
2.	-2 * 3 = -6	*The first number is negative and the second is positive*
	2 * -3 = -6	*The first number is positive and the second is negative*

Rules for the Division of Real Numbers
1. Divide the absolute values, if the signs are the same the result is positive
2. Divide the absolute values, if the signs are different the result is negative

Division Examples
1. 8 ÷ 2 = 4   *Both numbers are positive*
   -8 ÷ -2 = 4   *Both numbers are negative*
2. -8 ÷ 2 = -4   *The first number is negative and the second is positive*
   8 ÷ -2 = -4   *The first number is positive and the second is negative*

Rules for the Addition of Real Numbers
1. *Positive numbers*: Add the absolute value of the numbers. The answer is positive.
2. *Negative numbers*: Add the absolute value of the numbers. The answer is negative.
3. *A positive and a negative number*: Subtract the smaller absolute value from the larger. Then:
   a) If the greater absolute value was positive, the answer is positive.
   b) If the greater absolute value was negative, the answer is negative.
4. *One number is zero*: The sum is the other number.

Addition Examples
1. 2 + 3 = 5   *Both numbers are positive*
2. -2 + -3 = -5   *Both numbers are negative*
3. -2 + 3 = 1   *The first number is negative and the second is positive*
   2 + -3 = -1   *The first number is positive and the second is negative*
4. -2 + 0 = -2 or 2 + 0 = 2   *One number is zero*

Rules for the Subtraction of Real Numbers
1. *Positive numbers*:
   a) If the first number has the greater absolute value, the answer is positive.
   b) If the first number has the smaller absolute value, the answer is negative.
2. *Negative numbers*: Use the multiplication rule to change the second number to plus and then you will end up with an addition situation where you now apply the addition rule.
3. *A positive and a negative number*:
   a) If the second number is negative - Use the multiplication rule to change the second number to plus and then you will end up with an addition situation where you now apply the addition rule.
   b) If the second number is positive - add the absolute values the result will be negative.
4. *One number is zero*:
   a) If the first number is negative or positive the difference is the number.
   b) If the first number is 0 and the second number is negative, the result is positive value of the second number
   c) If the first number is 0 and the second number is positive, the result is the negative value of the second number.

Subtraction Examples

1. $5 - 3 = 2$ *The first number is bigger than the second number*
   $2 - 5 = -3$ *The second number is bigger than the first number*
2. $-2 - (-3) = -2 + 3 = 1$ *The second number is negative*
   $-5 - (-2) = -5 + 2 = -3$ *The second number is negative*
3. $2 - (-3) = 2 + 3 = 5$ *The second number is negative and the first number is positive*
   $-3 - 2 = -5$ *The second number is positive and the first number is negative*
4. a. $-2 - 0 = -2$ or $2 - 0 = 2$ *The second number is zero*
   b. $0 - (-2) = 2$ *The first number is zero*
   c. $0 - 2 = -2$ *The first number is zero*

(Hint: since the rules are given based on two numbers work with your numbers two at a time)

Operation Exercise

Find the absolute value for the following;
1) -5 2) 0 3) 75

Simplify the following;
4) $-3 - (-5) - 9 + 4 - (-6)$
5) $2(-4)^3 - 9(-10) + 3$
6) $30 \div \{5^2/(7-12)\} - (-9)$
7) $[37 + 15 \div (-3)]/2^4$
8) $13x - 5[10x - 7y - (3x - 15y)]$

Concept Application

1) **Purchase**: When you go to the store and is checking out, the cashier usually does not ring up your items in the same order that you put them on the counter. It does not matter which order the items are rang up your bill will be the same. What Property is being applied here?
2) **Purchase**: Say you are in a store and you have 3 items that cost $38 each how can you quickly estimate what your cost will be? What Property is being applied here?
3) **Purchase**: If you are purchasing 3 of the same items the cashier can either scan them one at a time or can scan one of the item and then hit a multiplier button and the total will be the same. What Property is being applied here?

Solutions at the end of this unit.

Solutions to Concept Application

1) *The commutative property.*
2) *You could quickly multiply $40 by 3 to get $120 then since $38 is $2 less than $40 multiply $2 by 3 to get $6 and then subtract $120 - $6 = $114. That is the distributive property.*
3) *The associative property.*

ALGEBRA MADE EASY UNIT 7
Fraction Notation

A *fraction* is a number that can represent part of a whole. A fraction consists of two parts a *numerator* and a *denominator*. The numerator represents the number of equal parts and the denominator tells how many of those parts make up a whole.

If two numbers are written in the form of $\frac{a}{b}$, then they are said to be in **Fraction Notation**, where 'a' ≠ 0 and 'b' ≠ 0. *(Recall that the sign "≠" means not equal to and that division by 0 is undefined.)*

Fraction Notation Example

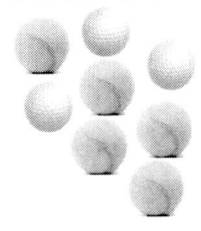

- In the given figure, 5 out of 8 balls are shaded.
- To write the fraction notation of the shaded part, we first note the numerator and denominator.
- Total number of parts will be written as the denominator.
- Number of parts that are shaded will be the numerator.
- Here, 5 out of 8 balls are shaded. So, 5 is the numerator and 8 is the denominator.
- So, we write the fraction as $\frac{5}{8}$

Least Common Denominator (LCD)

In order to add and subtract fractions that do not have the same denominator you need to know the LCD. The LCD or **least common denominator** is the smallest number that is a multiple of the denominators of two or more fractions.

Remember to first identify the denominator, the denominator is the number on the bottom of the fraction. For example if you have the fractions of 1/2 and 1/3, the denominators would be 2 for the 1/2, and 3 for the 1/3.

To find the **LCD** keep finding factors of both denominator until you have the same number for both.
2*1 = 2   3*1 = 3
2*2 = 4   3*2 = $\boxed{6}$
2*3 = $\boxed{6}$

Since 6 is the smallest number that both 2 and 3 can divide without leaving a remainder the LCD for 1/3 and 1/2 is 6.

Find the LCD of the following;
1) 1/5 and 1/4
2) 3/5 and 1/6
3) 8/9 and 1/3

> Solutions are at the end of this unit.

Adding Fractions

When adding fractions the denominators must be the same. If the denominators are not the same then you must first re-write the fractions as equivalent fractions using the **LCD** (*Least Common Denominator*) and then add them.

Equivalent fractions are two expressions that have the same value however they may have different appearances. *Example* 1/3 is equivalent to 2/6.

> Here are **3 Simple Steps to add fractions**:
> - Step 1: Make sure the bottom numbers (*the denominators*) are the same
> - Step 2: Add the top numbers (*the numerators*). Put the answer over the same *denominator*.
> - Step 3: Simplify the fraction (if needed).

Example – Same denominator

Add $\frac{3}{5} + \frac{1}{5}$

Solution
Since the denominator are the same

$$\frac{3}{5} + \frac{1}{5} = \frac{4}{5}$$

Example - Different denominator

Add $\frac{1}{2} + \frac{1}{3}$

Solution
The LCD = **6** (*The smallest number that both denominator can divide with no remainder*)
1/2 = 3/**6** and 1/3 = 2/**6** (*rewrite each expression as a new fraction using the new denominator*)
The expression now becomes 3/6 + 2/6 = **5/6**

Fractions Addition Exercise
Simplify the following;
1. 4/9 + 2/9
2. 6/15 + 4/15
3. 5/2y + 3/2y
4. 5/6 + 2/3
5. 8 + 7/26
6. 9/a + 5/2a

Subtracting Fractions

When subtracting fractions the denominators must be the same. If the denominators are not the same then you must first re-write the fractions as equivalent fractions using the LCD (Least Common Denominator) and then add them.

> Here are **3 Simple Steps to subtract fractions**:
> - Step 1: Make sure the bottom numbers (*the denominators*) are the same
> - Step 2: Subtract the top numbers (*the numerators*). Put the answer over the same *denominator*.
> - Step 3: Simplify the fraction (if needed).

Example – Same denominator: Subtract $\frac{3}{5} - \frac{1}{5}$

Solution

Since the denominator are the same

$\frac{3}{5} - \frac{1}{5} = \frac{2}{5}$

Example - Different denominator: Subtract $\frac{1}{2} - \frac{1}{3}$

Solution

The LCD = **6**   *(The smallest number that both denominator can divide with no remainder)*

1/2 = 3/6 and 1/3 = 2/6   *(rewrite each expression as a new fraction using the new denominator)*

The expression now becomes 3/6 - 2/6 = 1/6

Fractions Subtraction Exercise

Simplify the following;
1. 4/7 - 2/7
2. 6/25 - 4/25
3. 5/3y - 3/3y
4. 5/6 - 1/3
5. 6 - 7/25
6. 9/x - 5/3x

Multiply and Divide Fractions

Unlike addition and subtraction when multiplying and dividing fractions you do not need to find the LCD when the denominator as not the same.

Multiply Fractions

The multiplication of fraction is a four step process detailed in the chart.

> **When multiplying fractions**
> - **Step 1: multiply the numerator of one fraction with the numerator of the other**
> - **Step 2: Multiply the denominator of one fraction with the denominator of the other**
> - **Step 3: Put the new numerator on the top of the new denominator**
> - **Step 4: simplify the fraction (if needed).**

Example 1/3 • 1/2

Solution

$\frac{1}{3} \cdot \frac{1}{2} = \frac{1}{6}$ ⟵ *Multiply the numerator by the numerator*
       ⟵ *Multiply the denominator by the denominator*

The solution is 1/6

Fractions Multiplication Exercise

Simplify the following;
1. 4/5 * 2/7
2. 6/13 * 1/2

3. 5/6 * 1/6
4. 5/x * 3/3x

Divide Fractions
Division is the inverse of multiplication the steps are detailed in the chart.

> **When dividing fractions**
> - Step 1: Hold the first fraction fixed
> - Step 2: Change the sign of multiplication
> - Step 3: Invert the second (last) fraction
> - Step 4: Follow the rules given for multiplication.
>
> *(Since the steps are given based on two numbers it is best to work with two numbers at a time)*

Example 1/2 ÷ 2/3

Solution

1/2 • 3/2 ←——— *The second fraction is inverted*

The sign is changed

The solution is ¾

(Note that when working with fractions the order of operation and the rules of operation still apply.)

Fraction Division Exercise
Simplify the following;
1. 4/7 ÷ 2/7
2. 6/25 ÷ 4/25
3. 2/5 ÷ 3/5x
4. 5/6 ÷ 1/3
5. 6 ÷ 7/25

Concept Application
1) *Cooking:* Maisy prepares a mixed berry salad with 7/8 qt of strawberries, ¾ qt of raspberries, and 5/16 qt of blueberries. What is the total amount of berries in the salad?

Solution at the end of the unit.

LCD Answers
1) 1/5 and ¼; **LCD = 20**   2) 3/5 and 1/6; **LCD = 30**   3) 8/9 and 1/3; **LCD = 9**

Solutions to Concept Application
1) Total = 7/8 + ¾ + 5/16 = 14/16 + 12/16 + 5/16 = 31/16; The salad contains 31/16 quarts of berries.

ALGEBRA MADE EASY UNIT 8
Mixed Numbers

So far we have talked about whole numbers and we have talked about fractions. However there are still two other types of numbers that you will encounter. In this unit we are going to look at numbers that are made up of part whole number and part fraction.

First let's talk about the different types of fraction that you may encounter.

Types of Fraction

A Proper Fraction - The numerator is less than the denominator. *Examples are ¼, ¾, ⅜.*

An Improper Fraction - An Improper fraction has a top number larger than (or equal to) the bottom number. In other words it is "top-heavy". *Examples are 7/4, 3/2, 9/9.*

Mixed Numeral is a whole number and proper fraction together. An example is 2¾.

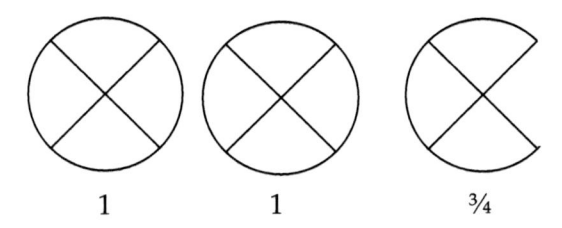

The *denominator* of the fraction tells how many pieces to separate the whole into. So since there are 2 wholes you have two complete circles separated into 4 sections. And since there is ¾ you have 3 sections of the third circle.

Writing an expression in mixed numeral is quite simple if you have **5** and **½** you write **5½**.

To convert a mixed numeral to a fraction is a bit more involved and is discussed next.

Converting Mixed Numeral To Fraction

Let's convert from a mixed numeral like 3⅝ to fraction notation:

$$3\frac{5}{8} = \frac{29}{8}$$

Steps
a) Multiply: $3 \cdot 8 = 24$
b) Add: $24 + 5 = 29$.
c) Keep the denominator; the result of above becomes the numerator.

3⅝ converted to fraction is $\frac{29}{8}$. *(Note that the result is an improper fraction.)*

To convert a fraction to mixed numeral **you divide** the numerator by the denominator. The result will be the whole number plus the remainder on top of the divisor. That is the divisor becomes the denominator.

Example 1: Convert 19/7 to mixed numeral

Solution

$$7\overline{)19} \quad \begin{array}{r}2\\14\\\hline 5\end{array} \rightarrow \text{The quotient} \qquad 2\tfrac{5}{7}$$

$\rightarrow$ The remainder

Conversion Exercise

Convert to an improper fraction
1) 6⅜   2) 8⅔

Convert the improper fraction to mixed numeral
2) 9/4   3) 174/8

Now let's look at operations involving mixed numerals.

Adding Mixed Numbers

Step 1: First add the whole numbers
Step 2: Then add the fractions. If the result is an improper fraction simplify by converting it to a mixed numeral.
Step 3: Combine the result of step 1 and step 2.

Example 2: Add 6⅜ + 3¾ and write the answer in mixed numeral

Solution
Step 1: 6 + 3 = 9
Step 2: ⅜ + ¾ = ⅜ + 6/8 = 9/6
Since 9/6 is an improper fraction we must convert it to a mixed numeral. That gives 1 & 1/8.
Step 3: the combined result is 9 + 1(1/8) = 10(1/8)

Add Mixed Numeral Exercise
Add and write the answer in mixed numeral
1) 4⅔ + 3(4/5)   2) 2(5/6) + 5(5/6)   3) 3(2/5) + 8(7/10)

Subtracting Mixed Numbers

Step 1: First subtract the whole numbers
Step 2: Then subtract the fractions. Note that you may need to *"borrow"* from the whole number. When you do that, use the denominator to help you re-write the one borrowed as a fraction
Step 3: Combine the result of step 1 and step 2.

Example 3: 9(5/6) – 2(1/6) and write the answer in mixed numeral

Solution
Step 1: 9 – 2 = 7
Step 2: 5/6 – 1/6 = 4/6
Step 3: The combined result is 7 + 4/6 = 7(4/6) = 7(2/3)

Example 4: 12 – 4⅔ and write the answer in mixed numeral

Solution
Step 1: 12 – 4 = 8
Step 2: First borrow 1 from 8; 8 = 7 + 1. Since there is a fraction with a denominator of 3 re-write the 1 as 3/3. 3/3 - ⅔ = 1/3
Step 3: The combined result is 7 + 1/3 = 7(1/3)

Subtracting Mixed Numeral Exercise
Subtract and write the answer in mixed numeral
1) 10(5/6) – 4(2/5)   2) 8(1/9) – 3(5/6)   3) -3(1/5) – 4(1/6)

Multiply Mixed Numeral

To multiply using mixed numerals do the following
Step 1: First convert to fraction notation.
Step 2: Then multiply with fraction notation, and, if appropriate, rewrite the answer as an equivalent mixed numeral.

Example 5: 4½ • 5/8

Solution
Step 1: 4½ = 9/2
Step 2: 9/2 • 5/8 = 45/16 = 2(13/16)

Multiply mixed numeral Exercise
Multiply the following and simplify your answer
1) 2(1/7) • 3(3/5)   2) 3(1/3) • 2½   2) 8 • 3½

Dividing Mixed Numeral

To divide using mixed numerals do the following
Step 1: First convert to fraction notation.
Step 2: Then divide with fraction notation, and, if appropriate, rewrite the answer as an equivalent mixed numeral.

Example 6: 6(1/4) ÷ 1(7/8)

Solution
Step 1: 6(1/4) = 25/4 and 1(7/8) = 15/8
Step 2: 25/4 ÷ 15/8 = 25/4 • 8/15 = 3(1/3)

Divide mixed numeral Exercise
Divide the following and simplify your answer
1) 2¼ ÷ 1(1/5)   2) 1¾ ÷ -2½

Application
1) *Cooking*: Dominique has a container containing 11/12 cup of grated Parmesan cheese and puts 1/8 cup on a her spaghetti and meatballs dinner. How much cheese remains in the container?

ALGEBRA MADE EASY UNIT 9
Decimals

The next types of numbers that we will look at are called *Decimals*. A number written in *decimal notation* is often simply referred to as a *decimal*. The word *decimal* comes from the Latin word *decima*, meaning a *tenth part*. Since our monetary system is based on tens, decimal notation is a natural extension of an already familiar system. The decimal point is represented by the dot in the number. For example the dot in $249.98 is called a **decimal point.**

PLACE–VALUE CHART							
Hundreds	Tens	Ones	Tenths	Hundredths	Thousandths	Ten-Thousandths	Hundred-Thousandths
100	10	1	$\frac{1}{10}$	$\frac{1}{100}$	$\frac{1}{1,000}$	$\frac{1}{10,000}$	$\frac{1}{100,000}$

The point value chart above helps with the placement of units. For example the decimal notation for 56.223 means   **5** tens + **6** ones + **2** tenths + **2** hundredths + **3** thousandths

Or $50 + 6 + \frac{2}{10} + \frac{2}{100} + \frac{3}{1000}$

To combine them simply find the LCD and add

$56 + \frac{2000}{1000} + \frac{200}{1000} + \frac{3}{1000} = 56 \frac{223}{1000}$

That is read as *Fifty-six and two hundredths and twenty three thousandths*.

Uses for decimal

As previously stated decimal notation is used with money. For example it is common on a check to write "and ninety-five cents" as "and $\frac{95}{100}$ dollars."

Example 1: Write $5876.95 in words, as on a check.

Solution
Five thousand, eight hundred seventy-six and $\frac{95}{100}$ dollars.

Convert from decimal to Fraction

Step 1: Count the number of decimal places,
Step 2: Move the decimal point that many places to the right, and
Step 3: Write the answer over a denominator of 1 followed by that number of zeros representing each place moved.

Example 2: Write 4.98 as a fraction and do not simplify your answer.

Solution

Step 1:   4.98   *There are 2 decimal places*

Step 2: 4.98   *Move 2 places to the right*

Step 3: $\dfrac{498}{100}$

Fraction Exercise
Write fraction notation for 0.925. Do not simplify.   (*Solution at the end of the unit*)

Adding Decimal

> Adding with decimal notation is similar to adding whole numbers.
> - First we line up the number in columns so that we can add corresponding place-value digits.
> - Add the digits from right to left.
> - If necessary, write extra zeros to the far right of the decimal point so that the number of places is the same for each of the numbers.

Example 3: Add: 4.31 + 0.146 + 15.2

<u>Solution:</u> Line up the decimal points and write extra zeros as place holder for missing digits.

```
   4.310
   0.146
  15.200
  ------
  19.656
```

Decimal Addition Exercise
Add the following;
1) 4576 + 17.892
2) –4.207 + (–3.851)
3) 1.06 + 9
4) 2.3 + 0.769 + 23

Subtracting Decimal

> Subtracting with decimal notation is similar to adding whole numbers.
> - First we line up the number in columns so that we can add corresponding place-value digits.
> - Subtract the digits from right to left.
> - If necessary, write extra zeros to the far right of the decimal point so that the number of places is the same for each of the numbers.

Example 4: Subtract: 34.07 − 4.0052

Solution

Line up decimal points and write extra zeros as place holder for missing. Then subtract, borrowing if necessary.

$$\begin{array}{r} 34.0700 \\ -4.0052 \\ \hline 30.0648 \end{array}$$

Subtraction Exercise

Subtract the following;
1) 36.2 − 16.28   2) 1 − 0.0098

Multiply Decimal Notation

Step 1: Ignore the decimal points temporarily and multiply as though multiplying integers.
Step 2: Locate the decimal point so that the number of decimal places in the product is the sum of the number of places in both numbers.
Step 3: Take the result of step 1 and put the point at the end. Count off the number of decimal places by starting at the far right and moving the decimal point to the left.

Example 5: 0.8×0.43

Solution

Step 1: 43 x 8 = 344
Step 2: In 0.8 there is 1 decimal point and in 0.43 there are 2 decimal points. Total number of decimal points = 1 + 2 = 3
Step 3: Take 344 and put the point at the end 344. Now move 3 places to the left
344. = 0.344

Multiplication Exercise

Multiply the following;
1) 7.3×85.1 2) 0.0042×3215 3) 5.7×0.9 4) 87×0.006

Multiply By Multiplies of 10

To multiply any number by 10, 100, 1000, and so on,
Step 1: Count the number of zeros and
Step 2: Move the decimal point that many places to the right. Use zeros as placeholders when necessary.

Example 6: 1000×34.45678

Solution

1000 × 34.45678   → 3 zeroes

1000 × 34.45678 = 34.456.78   → Move 3 places to the right.

1000 × 34.45678 = 34,456.78

Multiply By Multiplies of 10 Exercise
Multiply the following;
1) 100×5.1 2) $1000 \times (-2.3046)$

Dollars to Cents Conversion

To convert from dollars to cents you are multiplying by 100. Move the decimal point two places to the right and change the $ sign in front to a ¢ sign at the end.

Example 7: Convert $142.86 from dollars to cents.

Solution

$142.86 = 14,286¢   Move 2 places to the right.

The result is 14,286¢

Dollars to Cents Conversion Exercise
Convert the following from dollars to cents.
1) $189.64   2) $0.83

Division of Decimal

To perform long division by a whole number,
Step 1: Place the decimal point directly above the decimal point in the dividend, and
Step 2: divide as though dividing whole numbers.

The division process is not complete until there is a remainder of **0** or a **repeating pattern**.

Example 8: $7 \overline{)5.88}$

Solution

```
          0.84   ← Quotient
       7)5.88   ← Dividend
Divisor  560
          28
          28
           0    ← Remainder
```

ALGEBRA MADE EASY – A Practical Approach to Algebra

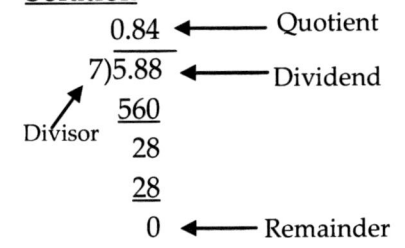

Example 9: 34 ÷ 8

Solution

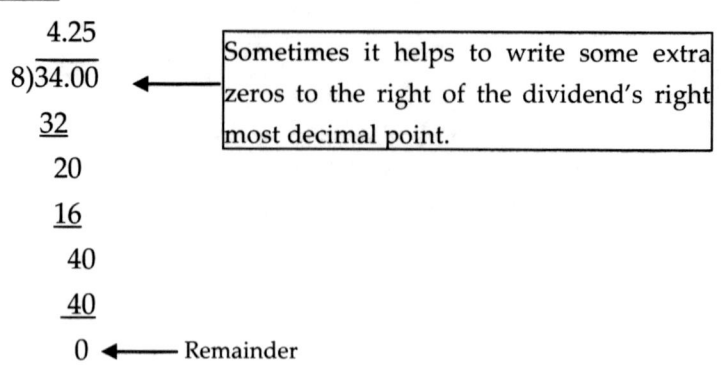

```
     4.25
  8)34.00
    32
    ---
    20
    16
    ---
     40
     40
     ---
      0  ← Remainder
```

Sometimes it helps to write some extra zeros to the right of the dividend's right most decimal point.

Example 10: 7 ÷ 40

Solution

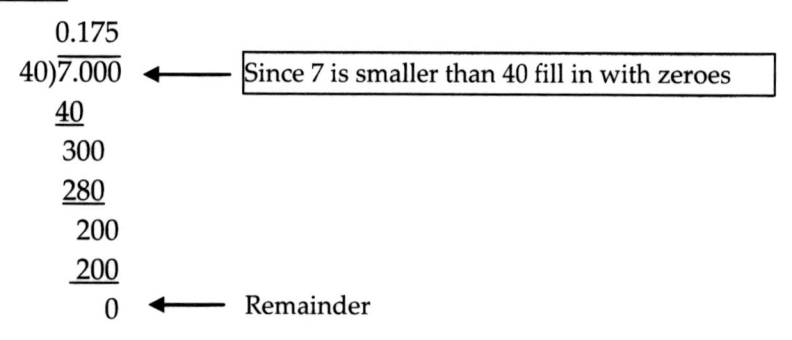

```
     0.175
  40)7.000
    40
    ---
    300
    280
    ---
     200
     200
     ---
       0  ← Remainder
```

Since 7 is smaller than 40 fill in with zeroes

Example 11: 1 ÷ 12

Solution

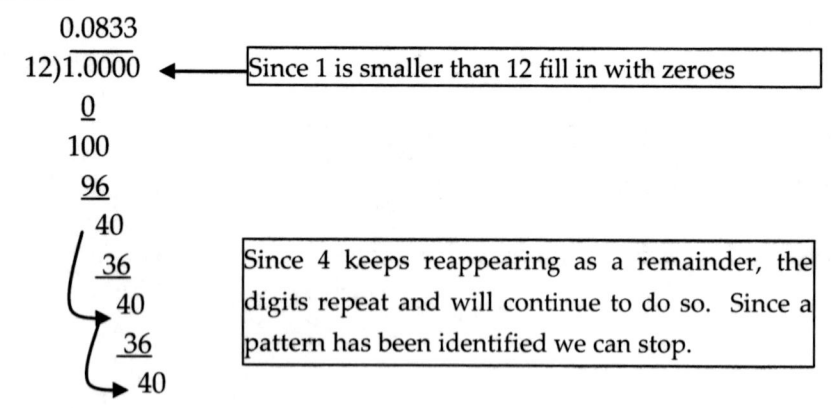

```
     0.0833
  12)1.0000
     0
     ---
     100
      96
     ---
       40
       36
      ---
        40
        36
       ---
         40
```

Since 1 is smaller than 12 fill in with zeroes

Since 4 keeps reappearing as a remainder, the digits repeat and will continue to do so. Since a pattern has been identified we can stop.

The result is 1 ÷ 12 = 0.0833…

The dots indicate an endless sequence of digits in the quotient. The dots are often replaced by a bar to indicate the repeating part.

Therefore $1 \div 12 = 0.08\overline{3}$

To divide when the divisor is not a whole number

Step 1: Start with the divisor. Move the decimal point (*multiply by 10, 100, and so on*) to make the **divisor** a whole number
Step 2: Move the decimal point the same number of places (*multiply the same way*) in the **dividend**
Step 3: Place the decimal point for the answer directly above the new decimal point in the dividend and divide as if dividing by a whole number

Example 12: $8.208 \div 0.24$

Solution

$$0.24\overline{)8.208}$$
→ Move 2 places to the right

Since there are 2 decimal places in 0.24. Multiply by 100 to make it a whole number.

$$\begin{array}{r} 34.2 \\ 24\overline{)820.8} \\ \underline{72} \\ 100 \\ \underline{96} \\ 48 \\ \underline{48} \\ 0 \end{array}$$

Decimal Division Exercise

Divide the following;
1) $91.26 \div 26$
2) $5.98 \div 2$
3) $7.872 \div (-9.6)$
4) $5 \div 11$

Division by Multiples of 10

To divide by a power of ten, such as 10, 100, or 1000, and so on,
Step 1: Count the number of zeros in the **divisor**, and
Step 2: Move the decimal point in the **dividend** that number of places to the left.

Example 13: $713.495 \div 100$

Solution

Step 1: There are 2 zeros in 100.
Step 2: 713.495 ← Move 2 places to the left

The result is 7.13495

Division by Multiples of 10th

> To divide by a tenth, hundredth, or thousandth, and so on,
> **Step 1**: Count the number of decimal places in the *divisor*
> **Step 2**: Move the decimal point in the dividend that number of places to the right.
> *(Essentially you are multiplying)*

Example 14: 89.12 ÷ 0.001

<u>Solution</u>
Step1: There are 3 decimal places in 0.001
Step 2: 89.12 → Move 3 places to the right

The result is 89,120

Division by Multiples of 10th Exercise
Divide the following
1) 0.3472 ÷ 10
2) -16.843 ÷ 0.001
3) 562 ÷ 100

Cents to Dollars Conversion

> To convert from cents to dollars you are dividing by 100. Move the decimal point two places to the left and change the ¢ sign at the end to a $ in front.

Example 15: Convert 8486¢ from cents to dollars.
<u>Solution</u>
8486¢ = $84.86 ← Move 2 places to the left.

The result is $84.86

Cents to Dollars Conversion Exercise
Convert the following from cents to dollars.
1) 343¢   2) 8503¢

> **Key Points**
> To determine whether or not an expression terminates or repeats consider the following;
> - When the denominator of a fraction has no prime factor other than 2 or 5, the decimal terminates. Example 7/40
> - If the denominator is a prime factor other than 2 or 5, the decimal repeats. Example 3/11

A *prime number* is a number that can only be divided evenly (*that is without a remainder*) by 1 and itself. Note that just because a number is odd does not mean that it is a prime number.

A *composite number* is any other number that is not a prime number. Note that 1 is neither composite nor prime.

Application Exercise

1) *Finance*: Colieman's cell phone plan consists of 450 anytime minutes and 1000 Night/ Weekend Minutes at a rate of $39.99. Additional anytime minutes are charged at a rate of $0.20 up to the next 50 minutes and $0.15 after that. Last month he used 600 anytime minutes and 800 Night/ Weekend Minutes. What was his cell phone bill for that period?

2) *Loan:* Maisy is purchasing a new computer for $2826. She is borrowing the money from the bank and wants to pay it back in equal monthly payments over two years. How much will she pay each month? *(Do not consider interest & fees)*

3) *Overtime Pay:* Nick earned $17 per hour for the first 40 hr of work and $25.50 per hour for work in excess of 40 hr. One week he earned $896.75. How much overtime did he worked?

4) *Service Calls*: H&L Service Center charges $30 for a house call plus $37.50 for each hour that the job takes. How long was spent on a house call where the bill was $123.75?

Fraction Exercise Answer
$$\frac{925}{1000}$$

ALGEBRA MADE EASY UNIT 10
Mathematical Expression

Math as a Symbolic Language
In math we represent thoughts and ideas using numbers, symbols and letters. We only have 9 digits and few symbols in addition to the letters that we borrow from the English language to convey our message. Think of a mathematical expression as a message that you are texting to your friend. Both you and your fiend must understand the symbols used so that you can send the message and your friend will understand it when the message is received. In algebra some of those symbols are pre-defined and you simply need to understand and use them.

Variables
Whenever we do not know a piece of information in algebra, it is the unknown, and we pick an alphabet to represent that unknown. Therefore a **variable** is a letter that represents a value. That value is more than likely going to be the answer that we are looking for. *(Note that it is important that when you chose the variable you declare it so that the receiver of your message will recognize it.)*

Mathematical Expression
The result of combining numbers and variables with ordinary arithmetic operations to represent an idea or a thought *(in other words your message)* is called an **expression.** You might even see it referred to as an **algebraic expression.**

Example 1
Translate the statement 2 times x into a mathematical expression.

<u>Solution:</u>
$2x$

Example 2
You have 2 green peppers, 1 red pepper, 2 yellow peppers, 3 granny smith apples, and 4 golden apples in your shopping cart.

Write the total number of apples and peppers that you have in your cart as an expression?

<u>Solution</u>
To write an expression we are going to use a variable to represent the items that we are talking about.
- Let **apples** be represented by *a*
- Let **peppers** be represented by *p*

The statement in algebraic expression is written as
$$2P + 1P + 2P + 3a + 4a$$
$$5P + 7a$$

This is without regards to the colors

Mathematical Equations

An **equation** is a statement of that combines two mathematical expressions. The expressions are combined using one of the following symbols (=, <, >, ≤, ≥).

For example
> In English you would say three times two equals to six.
> In Math you write **3 x 2 = 6**

Equation Example 1: Write the statements as equations.
> ***Three times a number is equal to six, what is that number?***

Solution
To answer this question you must realize that there are two sets of ideas that are expressed.

The first statement is ***Three time a number is equal to six***

Since we do not know the number you begin by picking a letter from the alphabet to represent the number.
- Let the number that you are looking for be some variable say x
Then the first statement can be written as **$3x = 6$**

The second statement is ***what is that number?***
> Using the variable that was defined, the second statement can be written as **x = ?**

So the response is ***Three times a number is equal to six, what is that number?*** Can be written as **3x = 6, x = ?**

In order to be able to provide the answer to questions we first translate that information to an expression, then formulate an equation and then solve that equation. It is the solution to that equation that will be the answer that we seek. We will be looking more at this later.

Expression & Equation Exercises
Translate into algebraic expressions
1. Nine less than some number
2. Half of a number
3. The difference of two numbers
4. One hundred less than the quotient of two numbers
5. Some number less than 10
6. Three times a number

> **Solutions to Concept Application**
> 1) Let Herm's rate of pay be x; then 38 * x = 1275; x = ?

Concept Application
Translate the following to an expression.
1) **Salary:** Serma earned $1275 this week and she worked for 38 hours. What is her rate of pay?

Solution at the right.

ALGEBRA MADE EASY UNIT 11
Test 1

1. Classify the number as one or more of the following: natural number, whole number, integer, rational number, or irrational number. (a) 5/3 (b) $\sqrt{16}$ (c) -200 (d) $\sqrt{12}$

2. Classify the number as prime or composite or neither. If the number is composite, write it as a product of prime numbers.   (a) 85   (b) 47   (c) 1   (d) 21

3. Solve (a) 25/0   (b) 31*-1   (c) 21*0   (d) 108/18

4. Evaluate the expression for $\dfrac{x^3 - 1}{2x}$, for $x = -2$

5. Translate the phrase *"four squared decreased by three"* to an algebraic expression. Then find the value of the expression.

6. Evaluate each expression. Write your answer in lowest terms.
   (a) ½ + 5/6   (b) 3/8 – 5/6   (c) 9/12 ÷ 3/8   (d) 1/3 * 4/5

7. Write as an exponential expression. (a) 4*4*4*4*4   (b) y*y*y*y

8. Find the value of y for the given values of x (a) $y = 2x - 2$; $x = 15$
   (b) $y = 4(2x - 1)$ for $x = 5$

9. Use multiplication to rewrite each expression, and then evaluate the result.
   (a) 2^3 (b) 9^0 (c) 6^1 (d) 3^4

10. Insert the symbol < or > to make each statement true. (a) 2 ☐ -5 (b) -8 ☐ -4

11. Evaluate the expression. (a) $2 + (8 - 20 \div 2^2) * 3$ (b) $6 \div 3 - 18 + 5 * 4$ (c) 4½ • 6⅔   (d) 5½ ÷ 2¾
    (e) 7.91 ÷ 10

12. State the property or properties that each equation illustrates.
    (a) 5 + (2 + 3) = (5 + 2) + 3   (b) 6x + 3 + 5x = 6x + 5x + 3   (c) 2 * (5*3) = 2 * 5*3

13. Simplify each expression. (a) $6x + 5x$ (b) $4x^2 + 2 - x^2$ (c) $3(2x - 1) + 5x + 10$

14. **Finance:** Kyle had an initial balance of $1258 in his savings account at the beginning of the month. Find the final balance in his account at the end of the month after the following transactions; Deposits of $2485, $350 and withdrawals of $115, $42.85, $475 and $183.

15. **Woodwork:** Jaden wants to make 66 wooden books. Each book will be 6 inches wide and 6 inches tall. How much feet of wood does he need to buy if the wood is already 6 inches wide?

16. **Cooking:** Maisy bought lunch meat for sandwiches. She purchased 2¼ pounds of ham, and 3⅔ pounds of turkey. How many pounds of lunch meat did she buy?

ALGEBRA MADE EASY UNIT 12
Rounding And Estimates

Have you ever had someone say to you or have you ever said to anyone *"how much do you think that this is worth?"* or *"Give me a ball park figure"*. If you have answered this question yourself or received an answer from anyone on a similar question then you were using the concept of estimating.

Estimating is an important part of mathematics and is another very handy tool that we use in our everyday life. We estimate things like money, time, distances, and many other physical quantities.

Rounding is a technique which involves looking at things in terms of whole numbers simply because as humans it is easier for us to work with whole number especially if you need to perform an operation quickly. There are a few rules regarding the rounding that we generally follow when doing calculations however as with everything else there are cases for deviation. Those case for deviation usually occur when working with real life situations; we will talk about those deviations as we encounter them.

Rounding

Generally speaking, when rounding if the digit is less than 5 you round down; if the digit is 5 or more you round up. You also need to consider what digit you are rounding to.

Example 1: Round 123 to the nearest ten

Solution
That means that you want to have no ones in the answer so you would look at the 3 and react based on whether or not it is 5 or greater or less than 5.

Since 3 is less than 5 that means that we round down and 123 becomes **120**.

Example 2: Round 126 to the nearest ten

Solution
That means that you want to have no ones in the answer so you would look at the 6 and react based on whether or not it is 5 or greater or less than 5.

Since 6 is greater than 5 that means that we round up and 126 becomes **130**.

Example 3: Round 125 to the nearest ten

Solution
That means that you want to have no ones in the answer so you would look at the 5 and react based on whether or not it is 5 or greater or less than 5.

Since 5 is exactly 5 that means that we round up and 125 becomes **130**.

Use a similar process to round to other digits.

Rounding Exercise
1. Round 625 to the nearest hundred
2. Round 86 to the nearest ten
3. Round 1368 to the nearest thousand

Estimating

We use estimating when we are trying to get an idea that is close to the value that we seek.

Example1. Given the following data estimate the following.

$85 $48 $299

1. Suppose you wanted to purchase two bikes how much money would you need to have? *Do not consider tax or any other fees.*
2. Suppose you wanted to purchase one train and one play house how much money would you need to have? *Do not consider tax or any other fees.*
3. Suppose you wanted to purchase one bike, one train and one play house how much money would you need to have? *Do not consider tax or any other fees.*
4. If you had $410 how many bikes could you purchase? *Do not consider tax or any other fees.*

Solution
1. Since each bike cost $85 you round up to $90 and your estimate is **$180**.
2. Since each train cost $48 you round up to $50 and since each playhouse cost $299 you round up to $300 and your estimate is $50 + $300 = **$350**.
3. Since each bike cost $85 you round up to $90, since each train cost $48 you round up to $50 and since each playhouse cost $299 you round up to $300 and your estimate is $90 + $50 + $300 = **$440**.
4. Since each bike cost $85 round up to $90 and then divide $410 by $90 to get 4.56 that means that you can purchase **4 bikes**. Note that even though 0.56 is closer to 1 than it is to zero since you cannot purchase a fraction of a bike you must round to the number that makes sense. *(This a case for deviation that was mentioned earlier.)*

Rounding and Estimate Exercise
1. Estimate 92.16 ÷ 25
2. Estimate 4.5 * 56
3. **Stocks**: When first listed a share of Facebook stock sold for $31, estimate the number of shares which can be purchased with $1000.

ALGEBRA MADE EASY UNIT 13
Exponents And Scientific Notation

Exponents
An exponent of 2 or greater tells how many times the base is used as a factor.
$$x * x * x = x^3$$

That means to multiply x by itself 3 times.

The **exponent** is 3 and the **base** is x.

An expression with a power is called **exponential notation**. The general format for *exponential notation* is given by

$$a^n$$

where a is the Base and n is the Exponent.

Example: What is the meaning of (a) 3^4 (b) $(3x)^3$

Solution
(a) 3^4 means $3 * 3 * 3 * 3$
(b) $(3x)^3$ means $3x * 3x * 3x$

When evaluating exponents here are two things to keep in mind
- $a^1 = a$ for any number a;
- $a^0 = 1$ for any nonzero number a

Example: (a) $10^0 = 1$
(b) $5^3 = 5*5*5 = 125$

Note that -2^2 is not the same as $(-2)^2$.
$-2^2 = -1 * 2^2 = -1 *2*2 = -4$
$(-2)^2 = -2 *-2 = 4$

Exponential Exercise
Evaluate the following without the use of a calculator:
1. 6^1
2. $(-4)^1$
3. 5^0
4. $(-8.2)^0$
5. 3^4
6. -4^2
7. 2^3
8. 4^2
9. $(-2)^3$
10. 5^3

Rules of Exponents

There are several rules for manipulating exponential notation to obtain equivalent expressions. We need to understand those rules in order to successfully carry out multiplication of polynomials. Let's look at the rules that we need to help with the calculations that we will be doing.

When multiplying exponents the bases must be the same: For example if you have
$$a^3 \cdot a^2 = (a \cdot a \cdot a)(a \cdot a) = a^5$$
3 factors   2 factors   5 factors

Here are a few rules that you always keep in mind
1 as an exponent: $\quad a^1 = a$
0 as an exponent: $\quad a^0 = 1, a \neq 0$

Product Rule

Since the word product indicates to multiply this leads to the *Product Rule*.

For any number *a* and any positive integers *m* and *n*,
$a^m \cdot a^n = a^{m+n}$
(When multiplying with exponential notation, the base must be the same, then keep the base and add the exponents.)

Example 1: Simplify $x^3 \cdot x^5$

Solution
$x^3 \cdot x^5 = x^{3+5}$ Adding exponents:
$\qquad\quad = x^8$

Product Rule Exercise
Simplify the following;
1) $6^2 \cdot 6^7 \cdot 6^3$ 　　　 2) $x \cdot x^6 \cdot x^9$ 　　　 3) $(w^3 z^4)(w^3 z^7)$

Quotient Rule

$$\frac{a^5}{a^2} = \frac{(a \cdot a \cdot a \cdot a \cdot a)}{(a \cdot a)} = a^3$$

Since the word quotient indicates to divide this leads to the *Quotient Rule*.

For any nonzero number *a* and any positive integers *m* and *n*,
$\dfrac{a^m}{a^n} = a^{m-n} \qquad a \neq 0$
(When dividing with exponential notation, the base must be the same, then keep the base and subtract the exponent of the denominator from the exponent of the numerator.)

Example 2: Simplify $\dfrac{x^9}{x^3}$

Solution
$\dfrac{x^9}{x^3} = x^{9-3} = x^6$

Quotient Rule Exercise
Simplify the following;

1) $\dfrac{6y^{14}}{6y^6}$ 2) $\dfrac{l^7 m^9}{l^3 m}$ 3) $\dfrac{5^9}{5^3}$

Power Rule

$(a^3)^2 = a^3 \cdot a^3 = a^6$ *(using the product rule you add the exponent)*

When an exponent is raised to another exponent we refer to it as an exponent to a power. This leads to the *power rule*.

> For any real number *a* and any integers *m* and *n*,
> $$(a^m)^n = a^{mn}$$
> *(When an exponent is raised to another exponent, multiply the exponents.)*

Power Rule Exercise
Simplify the following;
1) $(a^3)^2$ 2) $(4^2)^2$ 3) $(y^4)^5$

Raising A Product To A Power
Here is another expression that you might encounter in calculations
$(ab)^3 = a^3 \cdot b^3$

> For any real number *a* and *b* and any integer *n*,
> $$(ab)^n = a^n \cdot b^n$$
> *(To raise a product to the nth power, raise each factor to the nth power.)*

Example 3: Simplify $(2b)^3$
Solution
$(2b)^3 = 2^3 b^3 = 8b^3$

Product to Power Exercise
Simplify the following;
1) $(3x)4$ 2) $(-2x3)2$ 3) $(a2b3)7(a4b5)$

Raising A Quotient To A Power
Another expression that you might encounter is raising a quotient to a power.
$\left[\dfrac{a}{b}\right]^5 = \dfrac{a^5}{b^5}$

> For any real numbers *a* and *b*, $b \neq 0$, and any integer *n*,
> $$\left[\dfrac{a}{b}\right]^n = \dfrac{a^n}{b^n}$$
> *(To raise a quotient to the nth power, raise both the numerator and the denominator to the nth power.)*

Example 4: Simplify $\left[\dfrac{3}{4}\right]^3$

Solution

$\left[\dfrac{3}{4}\right]^3 = \dfrac{3^3}{4^3} = \dfrac{27}{64}$

Quotient to Power Exercise
Simplify the following;

1) $\left[\dfrac{w}{4}\right]^3$ 2) $\left[\dfrac{3}{b^5}\right]^4$ 3) $\left[\dfrac{a}{b}\right]^7$

Negative Exponent
For any real number *a* that is nonzero and any integer *n*,
$a^{-n} = \dfrac{1}{a^n}$

(*We will not discuss this in details since a polynomial cannot have negative exponents.*)

Scientific Notation

Scientific Notation is a form of exponential notation that is used for writing large numbers or very small numbers using a number from 1 to 9 followed by a decimal component and an exponent with a base of 10.

For example 543 can be written as 5.43×10^2

To convert a number to scientific notation look for the first non zero digit with a value between 1 and 9, put the point after it and then look to see how far you had to go either to the right or the left to get to that number and that will be the value of the exponent.

Example 1: Convert 61032 to scientific notation.

Solution
Since there is no decimal present assume the decimal to be at the end behind the 2
Keep moving left until there is only 1 digit with a value between 1 and 9 remaining

61032.   ← Move to the left

Count the number of digits that you passed to get to the 6, there were 4. That means that the exponent is 4. *Note that since the number was **greater than 1** and you had to move to the left the exponent is going to be positive.*

The result is 6.1032×10^4

Example 2: Convert 0.3265 to scientific notation.

Solution
Since there is a decimal present start there and move to the right unit there is a non-zero digit between 1 and 9.

$$0.3265 \rightarrow \text{Move to the right}$$

Count the number of digits that you passed to get to the 3, there was only 1. That means that the exponent is 1. *Note that since the number was **less than 1** and you had to move to the right the exponent is going to be **negative**.*

The result is 3.265×10^{-1}

Scientific Notation Exercises
Write the following in scientific notation:
1. 10593
2. 6798
3. 0.5635
4. 0.001065
5. The chance of winning the mega million lottery is one in a billion.

Concept Application
1) *Finance:* Maisy won last week's mega million lottery totaling three hundred and ninety six million dollars. Write that using scientific notation.

Solution at the end of this unit.

Solution to Concept Application
1) 1 million = 10^6
   Three hundred and ninety six million = $\$396 \times 10^6 = \$3.96 \times 10^2 \times 10^6 = \$3.96 \times 10^8$

ALGEBRA MADE EASY UNIT 14
Additive And Multiplicative Property

To solve equations we may sometimes to need to write the equation as equivalent equations. Equations with the same solutions are called **equivalent equations**. There are three main processes for solving equations and we will discuss two of them now. To **solve** a problem means that you end up with a relationship in relation to the other elements that were given.

To help us derive those equivalent expressions we are going to need to employ a few processes. The first of those processes is the **Additive Property** and since subtraction is the same as adding a negative number this process will apply whenever we need to add or subtract. The next process that we will talk about is the **Multiplicative Property** and since division is the same as multiplying by the reciprocal, this process will apply whenever we need to multiply or divide.

Additive Property (Also known as the Additive Principle)
The Addition Property of Equality states that; if A, B and C are real numbers, then the equations **A = B** and **A + C = B + C** are equivalent equations.

Simply put, that means that we can add the same number to both sides of an equation without changing the end result. Think of it as creating a balance scale.

Whatever I add on this side   I must also add to this side

Example
If Khal has a $1 bill and Rhea has 4 quarters; then Khal and Rhea have the same amount of money. This means that the value of $1 = the value of 4 quarters.

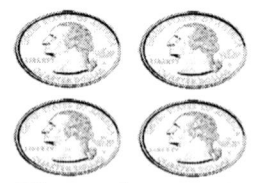

If C is a dime; and if I gave Khal a dime then must also give Rhea a dime so that in the end they will still have the same amount.
Then A + C = B + C are equivalent; that is the value of **$1 + dime = the value of 4 quarters + dime**.

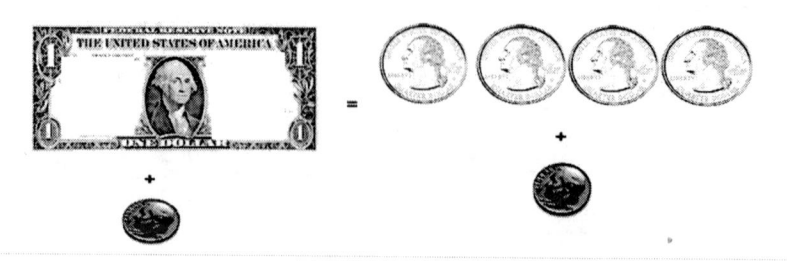

The final result is that in the end both Khal and Rhea will have the same amount of money.

Now let's look at this in a problem. *Example 1:* Evaluate $x - 5 = 2$ for x

Solution
$x - 5 + 5 = 2 + 5$ since in the original equation I was subtracting I must now add to isolate x
$\quad x = 7$
(Note that to get the answer you do the opposite of what was given in the equation)

Example 2: Evaluate $y + 7 = 6$ for y

Solution
$y + 7 - 7 = 6 - 7$ since in the original equation I was adding I must now subtract to isolate y
$y = -1$

Multiplicative Property (Also known as the Multiplicative Principle)
The Multiplication Property of Equality states that; if A, B and C represents real numbers and C is not equal to zero, then the equations **A = B and AC = BC** are equivalent equations.

In other words we can multiply each side of an equation by the same nonzero number without changing the solution.

Whatever I add on this side   I must also add to this side

Example, if Khal has a $1 bill and Rhea has 4 quarters; then they both have the same amount of money. That means that **the value of $1 = the value of 4 quarters**.

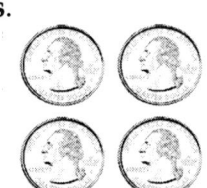

If I double the amount of money that Khal has then I must also double the amount of money that Rhea has to make sure that they will have the same amount of money. That means that the value of **$1 * 2 = the value of 4 quarters * 2**.

Now let's look at this in a problem. *Example 3:* solve $-x = 2$

Solution
$-x = 2$ Since I am looking for x and I have $-x$ I must multiply by -1 to get x.
$-x*-1 = 2*-1$
$x = -2$ (Since multiplying by -1 would give the same result as dividing by -1 here you could also divided also.)

Example 4: solve $2x = 28$

Solution
$2x = 28$ since in the original equation x is being multiplied by 2, I must
$(2x)/2 = 28/2$ divide by 2 to get x.
$x = 14$

Additive And Multiplicative Property Exercise
Solve the following:
1. $t - 3 = 19$
2. $x + ½ = -3/2$
3. $M + 18 = -13$
4. $6x = 90$
5. $-x = -10$
6. $2/3 = -5/6y$
7. $5x - 4 = 2x + 6$
8. $4x + 7 - 6x = 10 + 3x + 12$
9. $3x + 5 = 2(7x - 1)$
10. $8.4 - 3.2y = 4.24$

> Note: keep in mind that sometimes you might need to apply both properties in order to arrive at a solution. The key will be for you to determine which property to apply and when. Refer to the introduction when we talked about the toolbox approach.

Concept Application
1) *Budgeting*: Nick is in the tree preservation business. He can rent a tractor for $87.95 per day plus $4.25 an hour to assist in planting trees. He budgeted $120 per day for renting a tractor to plant trees on a job he is doing. The expression is given by *daily rate + cost per hour × number of hours = budgeted cost*. How many hours can Nick plant trees without exceeding the budget?

Solution at the end of this unit.

Solutions to Concept Application
1) daily rate + cost per hour × number of hours = budgeted cost
   $\$87.95 + \$4.25 \times h = \$120$
   $87.95 + 4.25h = 120$ Subtracting 87.95 from both sides
         $4.25h = 32.05$ Dividing both sides by 4.25
             $h = \frac{32.05}{4.25}$
             $h \approx 7.5$ Rounding to the nearest tenth

ALGEBRA MADE EASY UNIT 15
Linear Equations In One-Variable

Equations represent relationships and are used to find the answer to questions, therefore depending on the question that was asked the equation could contain one or more unknowns. The most distinguished characteristics of an equation are that the relationships given are equal.

Let's look at equations with **one** unknown.

A Linear Equation is one that is written using the "=" sign and is written in the form **ax + b = c**, where **a, b** and **c** are called **constants** and **a ≠ 0**. This is referred to a **linear equation in one variable**. If a = 0 and since *0*anything = 0* there will not be a question and as such you do not have an equation; instead you have a statement that could either be true or false. **Note that the x is a variable used to denote the unknown.**

Some examples of linear equations with one variable are as follows;
- $x + 8 = 0$
- $3x = 7$
- $x - 8 = 2$

Note that all of these equations can be written in the form ax + b = c.

Any replacement for the variable that makes an equation true is called a **solution** of the equation. To solve an equation means to find *all* of its possible solutions.

Example 1
Rhea bought 8 DVD's and gave some to Nick for his birthday gift. If Rhea has 5 DVD's remaining, how many did she give to Nick?

Solution
The unknown above is the number of DVD's that Rhea gave to Nick. So we will pick a letter to represent that unknown.

    Let the number of DVD's that was given to Nick be represented by **D**.
    The equation representing the information given above is **8 – D = 5**

Solving for D gives $D = 8 - 5 = 3$. **That means that Rhea gave Nick 3 of her DVD's.**

Example 2
Three times a number is 12; write an equation to state that information.

Solution
    Let the number that you are looking for be represented by x.
    The equation is **3x = 12**

Now take that a step further and find x. To do that, think back to the multiplicative principle.
    $(3x)/3 = 12/3$
    $x = 4$

Sometimes to solve an equation we may have several terms in our equations so let's look at the process of how we would combine those terms.

Like Terms
If two terms have the same variable, even if they are not the same value they are said to be alike. For example
> x and $2x$ are alike
> 4 and 3 are alike
> y and $0.5y$ are alike

Identify the like terms in the following?
1) $3xy - 5y + 2x - xy + 3y + 10$
2) $25a^2 + 6z + 4x^2 + 3a - 3z$

Solutions are at the end of this unit.

Combining Like Terms
When you get an equation you must first determine whether or not there are any terms that are alike and then combine them. To determine the like terms as you go through the problem use a methods to identify the things that are alike and then go back and combine them using the operation indicate.

Example: Combine the like terms in $2 - 3 + 5x + 7x + 6 - 2x$

Since I am writing I am going to use shapes to identify the things that are alike as I go through the expression.

⬜2 ⬜-3 ⭕(+5x) ⭕(+7x) ⬜+6 ⭕(-2x)

Note that the operation that is in front of the term goes with the term; if there is no operator given you assume plus.

Now combine all the circles and then combine all the squares.

The result is $5 + 10x$

When you are solving equations
- If like terms appear on the same side of an equation, combine them and then solve.
- If the terms appear on different sides, fist combine the like terms on each side. The use the Addition Principle to move all the terms with the variable that you are solving for to one side and put everything else on the other side.
    - Remember that when you solve an equation you are looking for the **variable = something.**

Example 1: Solve $2x + x = 9$

<u>Solution</u>
> $2x + x = 9$
> $3x = 9$
> $x = 3$

Example 2 Solve $2x - 2 = 9 - x + 1$

Solution

$2x - 2 = 9 - x + 1$

$2x - 2 = 10 - x$

$2x + x - 2 = 10 - x + x$

$2x - 2 = 10$

$2x - 2 + 2 = 10 + 2$

$2x = 12$

$2/2x = 12/2$

$x = 6$

Solving Linear Equations Tips

- ***Step 1:*** Simplify each side of the equation separately. Remember the order of operations.
- ***Step 2:*** Isolate the terms with the variables on one side of the equation. Use the addition property if necessary.
- ***Step 3:*** Isolate the variable. Use the multiplication property if necessary. Try to get the equation in the form x = something.
- ***Step 4:*** Check your answer. Substitute the value that you got back into the original equation and verify that the statement is true.

Example 3: Solve $2x - 15 = -4x + 21$

Solution

$2x + 4x - 15 = -4x + 4x + 21$

$6x - 15 = 21$

$6x - 15 + 15 = 21 + 15$

$6x = 36$

$6x/6 = 36/6$

$x = 6$

Linear Equations Exercise

1. $x - 25 = 30$
2. $m + 6 = 10$
3. $\frac{1}{2} = x - \frac{3}{4}$
4. $3x = 15$
5. $1 - 0.6x = 5$
6. $2x - 15 = -4x + 21$
7. $-4y - 15 = 25$
8. $2(x + 3) + 4x = 0$
9. $2(3y + 2) + 1 = 2(2y - 1)$
10. $-(y + 2) + (3y + 2) = -3(y + 1)$

Like Terms Exercise Answers

1) *The like terms are 3xy and – xy*
   – 5y and 3y
2) *The like terms are 6z and – 3z*

Solutions to Concept Application

1) *Let the total of the bill be x. The equations is 875 – x = 250; x = 875 - 250 = 625. The amount of her bill is $625.*

Concept Application

1) ***Finance:*** Serma got paid $875 and after paying her utility bill she has $250 remaining, how much was her bill?

ALGEBRA MADE EASY UNIT 16
Linear Inequalities

Numbers are written in order on the number line, increasing as we move from left to the right. For any two numbers on the line, the one to the left is *less than* the one to the right.

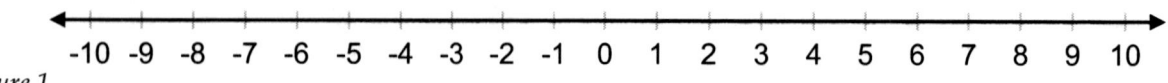

$$\xleftarrow{\quad\quad} -10\ -9\ -8\ -7\ -6\ -5\ -4\ -3\ -2\ -1\ 0\ 1\ 2\ 3\ 4\ 5\ 6\ 7\ 8\ 9\ 10 \xrightarrow{\quad\quad}$$

Figure 1

The symbol < means "is less than,"
7 < 8 is read "7 is less than 8."
-4 < -3 is read "-4 is less than -3."

The symbol > means "is greater than,"
5 > 4 is read "5 is greater than 4."
–6 > –7 is read "–6 is greater than –7."

Example 1
Use either "<" or ">" for ▢ to form a true sentence.
1) –7 ▢ 3   2) 8 ▢ –3   3) –21 ▢ –9

Solution
1) Since –7 is to the **left** of 3 we get –7 $<$ 3
2) Since 8 is to the **right** of –3 we get 8 $>$ –3
3) Since –21 is to the **left** of –9 we get –21 $<$ –9

Similar to Equations, Linear **Inequalities** also represent relationships and are used to find the answer questions. The most distinguished characteristic of an inequality is that the relationships given could result in more than one response. Think of inequalities as open ended questions.

An *Inequality* is a statement of that combines two expressions using the one of the following symbols;
<   >   ≤   ≥

Let's say that you have $10 and you are hungry, you are in the local deli and looking at the menu. What can you afford to buy?

Solution
You cannot spend more than you have therefore anything that you buy, plus the tax must be less than or equal to $10.
Some things that you would consider are as follows;
- Do you have to spend the entire $10?   **No**
- Can you spend a total of $10?   **Yes**

After answering those questions the conclusion is that what you can afford to buy can be represented by the following;

> Sandwich + Chips + Drink <u>less than or equal to</u> $10
> Sandwich + Chips + Drink $\leq$ $10

Example 1: Driving: Colieman is going to work and the speed limit on I-275 is 75 mph. As long as Colieman's speed stays below 75 he is not speeding and should not get a ticket. Write Colieman's speed as an inequality.

<u>Solution</u>
Colieman's speed can be 75 and below and can be represented by

> Speed $\leq$ 75

That means that Colieman's speed is anywhere between 0 and 75 he should not get a ticket.

Example 2: Baking: Maisy is baking cupcakes for her fifth grade students. She had 20 students that are regular and a few students that attend periodically. Write the number of cupcakes that Maisy need to have as an inequality so at each of the regulars gets a cupcake.

<u>Solution</u>
First we need to note that since there are 20 regulars she needs to have at least one for each child therefore the least amount of cupcakes that she can have is 20. Since she has a few that show up un-announced she might want to bake a few extra.

Therefore the number of cupcakes that Maisy needs is represented by

> Cupcakes $\geq$ 20

That means that Maisy will bake 20 or more cupcakes.

Equations Vs. Inequality

The processes for solving inequalities are the same as the processes for solving equations. That is the addition and the multiplication properties are applied in much the same ways with one difference with the multiplication property. When you divide an inequality by a negative number the sign changes.

Equation Example solve $3x = 6$ for x.

<u>Solution</u>
> $3x/3 = 6/3$
> $x = 2$ *In this case there is only one value for x and that is 2.*

Inequality Example 1: Solve $3x < 6$ for x

<u>Solution</u>
$3x/3 < 6/3$
$x < 3$ In this case x can be any value that is less than 3. For example x could be 2, it could be 1 or it could be 0.

Inequality Example 2: Solve $2x + 2 > 11 + 5x$ for x

<u>Solution</u>
$2x + 2 > 11 + 5x$
$2x - 5x > 11 - 2$
$-3x < 9$
$x > 3$ ← Note that the sign changes

When you divide an inequality by a negative number the sign of the inequality is reversed.

<u>Linear Inequalities Exercise</u>
Solve each inequality
1) $2x - 7 < -1$
2) $5 - 3x < 11$
3) $½x - ⅔ \leq x + ¾$

4) **Lunch:** Serma has $20 and is going to purchase lunch she also needs to have at least $1.50 for her bus rider home and another $3.50 for the cab ride from the bus stop to her door. How much can Herm spend on her lunch?

5) **Purchases:** Kim plans to spend $500 or less on an electrical dryer. There is a 9% sales tax and $64 setup/delivery charge that she needs to consider.
What price dryer can Kim really afford?

6) **Home Sale:** Dominique owns a home which needs to sell. She currently owes the bank $142,000 and the real estate agent gets a commission of 6%. How much must Dominique sell the house for to make sure that she has at least enough money to pay off the bank loan after the sale?

ALGEBRA MADE EASY UNIT 17
Introduction To Problem Solving

In mathematics we use a combination of expressions and operation to help us arrive at a solution. Therefore when you are asked a question you must first translate the meaningful data into an equation or an inequality and then carry out the indicated operation. Once you've carried out the operation; you then state the answer to the question. This is important; simply doing the calculations is not enough you must answer the original question that was asked. The person that asked the question might not know what the variable that you used in the calculation represents.

In this unit we are going to practice translating information into equation and the solving those equations to get answers. We are going to practice solving word problems.

Remember that equations and inequalities represent relationships and the solution that you are looking for is represented by the unknown (indicated by the variable).

> **Tips for solving Word Problems**
> *Step 1:* First read the problem through once to familiarize yourself with it. (*This is very important since more than likely this is the first time that you are seeing the question.*)
> *Step 2:* Then read it through a second time; this time take note of the information that you have been given (*the known*) and what you have been asked to do (*the unknown*).
> *Step 3:* Read the problem a third time, keeping in mind what you have been given and what you have been asked to do and "start to plan" (*determine a method*) how you are going to get to the solution.
> *Step 4:* It always helps the read the problem though one last time to ensure that you understand the information.

Example
John works 15 hours per week and his weekly salary is $300, how much does John earn per hour?

<u>Solution</u>
Step 1- Read the problem through once to familiarize yourself with the contents.
Step 2 - Then read a second time, this time noting the information that you were provided
>John works 15 hours per week
>His weekly wages is $300
>Unknown: - His hourly wages (*rate per hour – that is what you were asked to find*)

Step 3 - On the third read I am going to start thinking of how to determine John hourly wages. **I am going to let his hourly wages be 'w' and set up an equation.**

Step 4 - Read the problem though one last time to ensure that you understood the information that was given, what you were asked to calculate and verify that you chose the correct approach.

Now that you have read and understood the information proceed to set up the equation and carry out the calculations to arrive at a solution.

Setting up the Equation
What you are missing is the relationship between the weekly salary, the number of hours worked and the pay rate.

Some relationship will be provided in the problem; others you are expected to know. Hopefully, you are aware that to find out how much one's salary is you multiply the number of hours worked by the hourly wages. That is the **relationship** (*also known as the formula*) that you will need to solve this problem.

Let the hourly wages be W.
The relationship is **Wages x Hours Worked = Salary**
$$W \times 15 = 300$$

Since W is the unknown when we solve for (or find) W we will have our answer.

$$\frac{W \times 15}{15} = \frac{300}{15} \quad \text{(divide both sides of the equation by 15)}$$
$$W = 20$$

Now the answer to the question that was asked is **John earns $20 per hour**.

The only way to get better at solving work problems is to practice, practice, and practice.

Problem Solving Exercises
1) *Finding Age:* In 10 years, a child will be 3 years older than twice her current age. What is the current age of the child?
2) *Medicare Enrollment:* In 2004, 41.2 million people were enrolled in Medicare, an increase of 5.1% from 2000. How many people were enrolled in Medicare in 2000? (*Source:* Health Care Financing Administration.)
3) *Salary:* A part-time instructor is receiving $950 per credit taught. If the instructor receives a 4% increase, how much will the new per credit compensation be?
4) *Saline Solution:* A solution contains 3% salt. How much water should be added to 20 ounces of this solution to make a 1.2% solution?
5) *Parking Rates:* Parking in a student lot costs $2.50 for the first hour and $1 for each hour thereafter. A nearby lot costs $1.25 for each hour. In both lots a partial hour is charged as a full hour. In which lot can a student park the longest for $5? For $11?
6) *Revenue and Cost:* The cost to produce one compact disc is $1.50 plus a one-time fixed cost of $2000. The revenue received from selling one compact disc is $12.
    (a) Write a formula that gives the cost C of producing x compact discs. Be sure to include the fixed cost.
    (b) Write a formula that gives the revenue R from selling x compact discs.
    (c) Profit equals revenue minus cost. Write a formula that calculates the profit P from selling x compact discs.
    (d) What numbers of compact discs need to be sold to yield a positive profit?

ALGEBRA MADE EASY UNIT 18
Formula And Problem Solving

A formula is a relationship or type of pattern between two things. We use formulas in math to help us answer questions or solve problems. The relationship can be interchangeable depending on the circumstance. As a result when you **solve** a formula you might not end up with a numeric value; instead you could end up with another relationship.

For example when a person is born they are the child and as such are dependent on their parent. In this case the child is the dependent party in this relationship and the parent is the independent party. Now when the child grows up and have a child of his or her own the situation has changed and the child is now the independent party and their child is now the dependent party.

Similarly in math the position of a variable can change dependent on the situation given. Therefore it is always important to know what you were asked to find.

For example the area of a square is given by the formula $A = L * W$. If you were given the width of a square as **3 units** and length as **4 units** and asked to find the area, you would use the formula $A = L * W$, substitute values for L and W and calculate to find A.

$A = 3 * 4 = 12$ Squared units

Now let's say that you were given the **Area as 15 squared units** and the **length as 5 units** and asked you to find the **width**. You would have to solve the formula for W to get $W = A/L$ then substitute for A and L to find W. $W = 15/5 = 3$ **units**.

Note that in both examples the same formula was used however the position of the variable changed depending on the information that was given and what you were asked to solve for.

To write a formula in terms of a specific variable you do that by solving the formula for that variable. (*Refer to the additive and multiplicative properties for solving equations.*)

Formula Exercises
Solve for the following variables;
1. $C = (F - 32)*5/9$ for F
2. $2a = 4b + c/2$ for c
3. $A = \pi * r^2$ for r

Problem Solving
Word problems tend to be a challenge for a lot of students. Refer to unit 17 to see how to go through the process of translating the information given into an equation or an inequality. As you saw once the information was translated into an expression or an equation, *essentially a formula was created*, we could then solve for the unknown which in that example was John's rate of pay.

In most problem solving situations if the relationship relates to everyday activities such as shopping, you will not be given the relationship or a formula however you are expected to know it. In some cases if it is basic information which everyone is expected to know you might not be given it either. If you do not know a relationship and it was not given stop and research it.

Life is not perfect so when it comes to problem solving you will have to apply reasoning and logic to set up the relationship based on the information that is given. Do not simply force the formula into the problem; you might have to make slight adjustment for it to work for the particular situation.

Some common relationship that you are expected to know are as follows;
- Pay Amount = Hours Worked × Rate of Pay
- Total Sales = Purchase + Applicable Tax + Applicable Service Fee (*where appropriate*)
- Tax = Amount × Tax Rate
- Sale Price = Original Amount – Discount
- Discount = Original Amount × Discount Rate

Problem solving is the core of our everyday lives so you should practice until you become proficient. If you think about it you do some amount of problem solving every day; whether it is a purchase that you are about to make or a task that you need to accomplish at work or at home. Use the exercise given to practice.

Problem Solving Exercises
Determine the relationship (*find the formula*) and then solve.
1. *Discount:* A couch marked $875 is on sale for 25% off. What is the discount? What is the sale price?
2. *Sale:* A coat is on sale for 25% off the list price and the price on the tag is $87. What was the price of the coat before it went on sale?
3. *Investment:* Find the amount in an account if $2000 is invested at 3%, compounded weekly for 1 year.
4. *Discount:* A local store have a sale going on buy 2 any signature collection item get 1 or Buy 3 get 2. They also have a coupon for $10 off $30 or more. Jessica went in the store to purchase a bottle of lotion and a bottle of body wash and saw the sale. Jessica was only planning to spend $21 help her determine the best decision base on the promotions that are available.
    - A bottle of lotion cost $10.50
    - A bottle of body wash cost $10.50
5. *Sales:* Let's say that you saw an item on sale at two different stores. **Store A** store has a sign that reads "**20% of the original price**". The original price was **$60.00**. **Store B** has a sign that reads **Current Sale Price $50 Take an Additional 10% off**. The original price **$55.00**. Which store is giving the better deal?
6. *Distance Traveled:* A bicyclist is 4 miles from home, riding away from home at 8 miles per hour.
    (a) Use the information above to find the distance D from home after 0, 1, 2, 3, and 4 hours.
    (b) Write a formula that calculates D after t hours.
    (c) Use your formula to determine D when $t = 3$ hours. Does your answer agree with the valued found in part a?
    (d) Find t when $D = 22$ miles. Interpret the result.

ALGEBRA MADE EASY UNIT 19
Test 2

1) Estimate the cost of purchasing two ragdolls $39.95

2) If I have $1500 how much swing set and ragdolls could I buy? $399.9

3) Evaluate the following without the use of a calculator:
   (a) 25^0 (b) 9^1 (c) $(-5.8)^0$

4) Convert 3965 to scientific notation.

5) Convert 0.0056 to scientific notation.

6) $x + 25 \leq 55$

7) $3 + 2x = 5 + x$

8) **Investment:** Vivienne bought 300 shares of Facebook at $31.00 per share. When she sold a share of Facebook went for $19.85. What is her net gain or loss for owning the shares?

9) **Solution Mixture:** A solution contains 15% hydrochloric acid. How much water should be added to 50 milliliters of this solution to dilute it to a 2% solution?

10) **Parking Rates:** Parking in a student lot costs $2 for the first half hour and $1.25 for each hour thereafter. A partial hour is charged the same as a full hour. What is the longest time that a student can park in this lot for $8?

ALGEBRA MADE EASY UNIT 20
Geometry

Geometry
In this unit we will look at geometry and its importance in helping us to solve problems. When asked certain questions, the only way to arrive at a response is to relate it to something that we know. That is the importance of geometry.

A **geometric figure** is simply a set of points.

A **segment** is a geometric figure consisting of two points, called *endpoints*, and all points between them.

A **line** is one of the basic shapes in geometry and is formed by a point moving along a fixed path.

Basic Shapes
At this time we will only look at a few basic shaped and some basic formulas. We are not going to derive these formulas we are going to state them and use them going forward.

A **Triangle** is a closed three sided figure. See the picture below for one shape of a triangle.

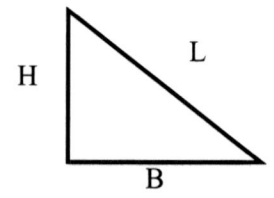

Dimensions of the Geometric Figure
If a walking path is triangular in shape and you wanted to know the total distance travelled after walking one lap, you would add all the sides together. That is called the *perimeter*. Thus the formula for finding the perimeter of a triangle is $L + B + H$.

$P_{triangle} = L + H + B$

Example: Find the perimeter of the given triangle.

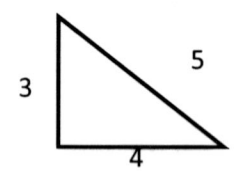

Solution
$P = L + H + B$
$3 + 4 + 5 = 12$ units

Perimeter is one dimensional and is thus measured in single units.

If you wanted to plant some grass in the center of that path you would need to find the dimension of the inner section between the lines; that is called the *area*. The area of a triangle is given by ½b*h (*where h is the perpendicular height*).

$$A_{triangle} = \frac{1}{2} b*h$$

Example 1: Find the area of the triangle given.

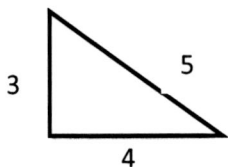

Solution
$A = ½ * b * h$
   $= ½*4*3 = 12/6 = 2$ squared units

Area is two dimensional and is thus measured in squared units.

A **Rectangle** is a closed four sided figure. See the picture below.

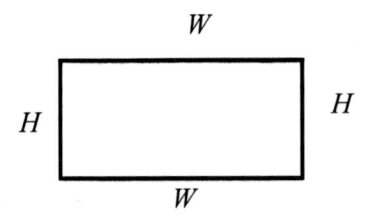

If a walking path is rectangular in shape and you wanted to know the total distance travelled after walking one lap you would add all the sides together. That is called the *perimeter*. Thus the formula for finding the perimeter of a rectangle is $L + W + L + W = 2L + 2W = $ **2(L + W)**.

$$P_{rectangle} = 2(L + W)$$

Example 2: Find the perimeter of the rectangle given.

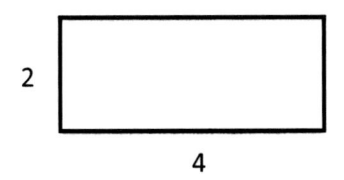

Solution
$P = 2(L+W)$
   $= 2*(2 + 4)$
   $= 2 * 6 = 12$ units

If you wanted to plant some grass in the center of that path you would need to find the size of the section enclosed between the lines. That is called the *area*. The area of a rectangle is given by $L * W$.

$$A_{Rectangle} = L * W$$

Example 3: Find the area of the rectangle given.

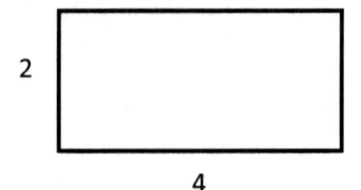

(rectangle with width 2 and length 4)

Solution
$A = L * W$
   $= 2 * 4 = 8$ squared units

A **Square** is a closed four sided figure, much like a rectangle with the only exception is that all of its sides measure the same. See the picture below.

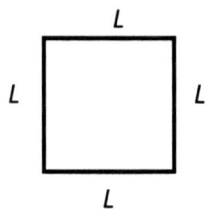

(square with all sides labeled L)

If a garden is squared shape and you wanted to know how much fence it would take to enclose it you would add all four sides. Thus the formula for finding the perimeter of a square is $L + L + L + L = 4L$.

$P_{square} = 4L$

Example 4: Find the perimeter of the square given.

(square with side 15 m)

Solution
$P = 4L$
Length = 15
Perimeter = $4L = 4 \cdot 15 = 60$
The answer is 60m.

If you wanted to plant some grass in the center of that garden you would need to find the size of the section enclosed within the fence. That is called the *area*. The area of a square is given by $L * L = L^2$.

$A_{square} = L^2$

Example 5: Find the area of the square given.

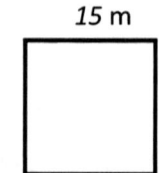

(square with side 15 m)

Solution
$A_{square} = L^2 = 15^2 = 225$
The answer is 225m².

Note that there are other shapes with four sides that are not covered in this material.

A **Circle** is a closed line that forms a round figure. See the picture below.

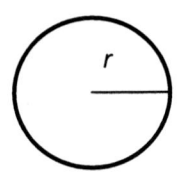

The distance around the circle is the perimeter; however it is also called the *circumference*. The formula for finding the circumference of a circle is **2πr**.

$$C = 2\pi r$$

The formula for finding the *area* of a circle is given by **πr²**.

$$A_{circle} = \pi r^2$$

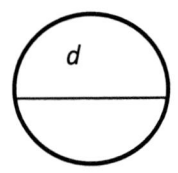

The *diameter* is the distance across from one edge of the circle, through the center to the next edge. The radius is the distance from the center of the circle to the edge of the circle. The *radius* is one half of the diameter therefore the diameter is given by **2r**.

$d = 2r$ or $r = d/2$
Since $C = 2\pi r$ and $r = d/2$
Then $C = \pi d$

π is a constant and has a numerical value of 22/7 or 3.14. You will be expected to know this information going forward.

Example 4: Find the diameter of the given circle

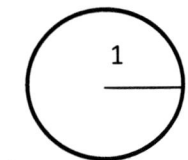

Solution
$d = 2r$
$= 2 * 1 = 2$ units
Diameter and radius are one dimensional and are thus measured in single units.

Example 5: Find the circumference and area of the given circle

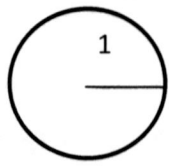

Solution
$C = 2\pi r$
　$= 2 * 3.14 * 1$
　$= 6.28$ units

Circumference is one dimensional and is thus measured in single units.

$A = \pi r^2$
　$= 3.14 * 1 * 1$
　$= 3.14$ squared units

Application Example

As you go through word problems you want to consider what geometric figure the scenario in your problem represents, and then use what you know about that geometric figure to help you to answer the question that was asked.

Example 6: Gardening: Colieman is going to put edging around a square flower bed 10 feet by 8 feet. The edging costs $5.95 per foot. How much would it cost Colieman to buy the edging for this project?

Solution
Thoughts
1. The first thing that you would do is find out how much edging you are going to need. Do this by choosing the geometric shape that represents the flower bed.
2. The next thing that you would ask your self is how to find out the distance around that figure.
   - The shape is a square
   - You need to find the perimeter. Now use the formula for the perimeter of a square to find the distance around the flower bed.

$P = 2(L + W)$
　$= 2(10 + 12)$
　$= 2(22)$
　$= 44$

Now that you know that the distance around the garden is 44ft; the final thing is to ask yourself how to find out the cost of 44 ft if the cost of 1ft is $5.95.
   - Now multiply 44 ft by $5.95 to get the total cost for the edging.

　　$44 * 5.95 = 261.8$

Therefore it will cost Colieman about **$261.80** to put the edging around the garden.

Example 7: A rectangular room has a perimeter of 80 and length 25m. Find the width of the room.

Solution

Step 1: Read the question and make sure that you understand the information that you have been given and what you have been asked to do. $P = 80$ and $L = 25$.

Step 2: You were asked to find the width of the room, so choose a variable to represent the width. If you need to, draw a picture. **Let the width be W.**

Step 3: Pick an equation to use. Think what shape the room is and what dimension link the perimeter, width and length together for that shape.

Use the formula for the perimeter of a rectangle, $P = 2L + 2W$
$80 = 2(25) + 2W$
$80 = 50 + 2W$

Step 4: Solve the equation for W
(Note that you will have to refer to the process that you learned for solving equations.)
$80 - 50 = 50 - 50 + 2w$
$30 = 2w$
$30(½) = 2w(½)$
$15 = w$

Step 5: State the answer
The width of the room is 15m

Step 6: Check your answer by using the length and the width to find the perimeter. $P = 2L + 2W$
$P = 2(25) + 2(15)$
$P = 50 + 30$
$P = 80$ *checks*

Surface Area

A rectangle is made up of six sides three of which are identical to each other. If you wanted to find out how much gift wrap paper it would take to wrap the box shown below then you would need to know how much paper it would take to cover each side; that is its surface area. The **surface area** of a rectangular solid with length l, width w, and height h is given by the formula $SA = 2lw + 2lh + 2wh$ or $2(lw + lh + wh)$.

$SA = 2lw + 2lh + 2wh$, or $2(lw + lh + wh)$

Example 8: Find the surface area of the rectangular solid.

Solution
$SA = 2lw + 2lh + 2wh$
$= 2(12 \text{ m})(10\text{m}) + 2(12\text{m})(9 \text{ m}) + 2(10\text{m})(9\text{m})$
$= 240 \text{ m}^2 + 216 \text{ m}^2 + 180 \text{ m}^2$
$= 636 \text{ m}^2$
The surface area of the solid is 636 m².

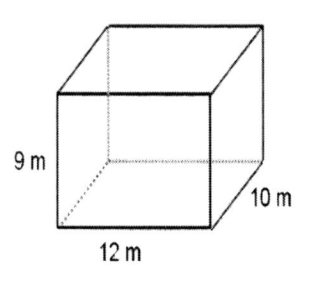

Volume

The **volume of a rectangular solid** is found by multiplying the length by width by height:

$V_{solid} = l*w*h$

Example 9: **Food**: Find the volume of the popcorn that it will take to fill the container. The bag measures 10 in. by 5 in. by 6 in.

Solution
$V = l*w*h$
$V = 10 * 5 * 6 = 300$ in³. **It would take 300 cubic inches of popcorn to fill the bag**.
Note that volume is measured in cubic units.

The volume of a circular cylinder is found in a manner similar to finding the volume of a rectangular solid—it is the product of the base area and the height. The height is always measured perpendicular to the base.

The **volume of a circular cylinder** is the product of the base area B and the height h given by;
$V = B*h$ or $V = \pi * r^2 * h$

Example 10: Find the volume water that it would take to fill this circular cylindrical drum. Use 3.14 for π.

Solution
$V = \pi * r^2 * h$
$ = \pi * r^2 * h$
$ = 3.14 * 25 * 18$
$ \approx 1413$ cm³
    It would take 1413 cm³ of water to fill the drum.

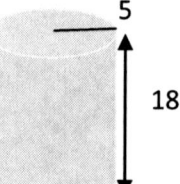

Sphere

A **sphere** is the three-dimensional counterpart of a circle. It is the set of all points in space that are a given distance (the radius) from a given point (the center). The volume of a sphere depends on its radius.

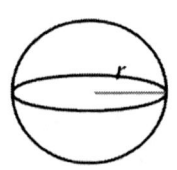

The **volume of a sphere** of radius r is given by $V_{sphere} = 4/3*\pi*r^3$

*Example 11: **Sports**:* The radius of a standard women's basketball is 4 inches. Find the volume of air that it would take to fill the standard-sized basketball. Round to the nearest hundredth cubic inch.

Solution
$V = 4/3*\pi*r^3$
$ = 4/3 * 3.14 * 4^3$
$ \approx 267.95$ in³   **It would take 267.95 cubic inches of air to fill the ball.**

Cone

The **volume of a circular cone** with base radius r is one-third the product of the base area and the height.

$$V_{cone} = 1/3 \; \pi * r^2 * h$$

Example12: Find the volume of ice-cream that it would take to fill cone shown. Only fill the cone to the rim.

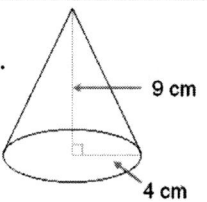

9 cm
4 cm

Solution
$V = 1/3 \; \pi * r^2 * h$
$\approx 1/3 * 3.14 * 4^2 * 9$
$\approx 150.72 \; cm^3$ **It would take 150.72 cm^3 of ice-cream to fill the cone.**

Geometry Exercises
1. Find the area of the given shape

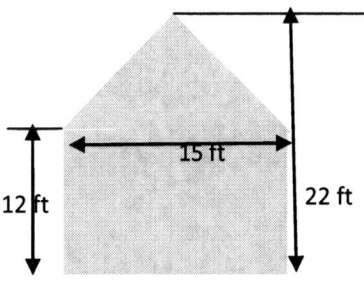

   15 ft
   12 ft
   22 ft

2. *Farming:* A farmer wishes to fence in a pasture for his goats. The pasture is 75 feet by 120 feet. How many feet of fence will be needed? If fencing sells for $3.95 per feet, what will the fencing cost?

3. *Home Improvement:* In order to save energy Serma plans to run a bead of caulk sealant around 3 exterior doors and 13 windows. Each window measures 3ft by 4 ft and each door measures 3 ft by 7 ft. Each cartridge of caulk seals 56 ft and cost $5.95. How much will it cost Serma to complete the job?

4. *Exercise:* A walking trail has the follow shape shown. How far would you have walked after one lap?

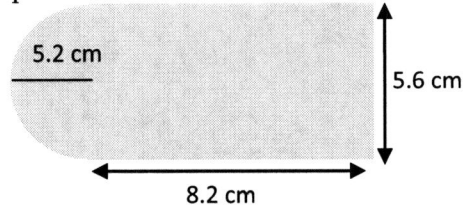

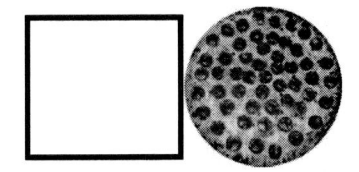

   5.2 cm
   5.6 cm
   8.2 cm

5. *Pizza:* A local pizza parlor is ordering new square serving boxes. They want to know if they will have enough space left over to include garlic sauce with each pizza. If they order a 16 in. box how much area will left over when a 14 in. diameter pizza is placed on the box?

6. *Bowling Ball:* The radius of a standard-sized bowling ball is 4 in. Find the volume of a standard-sized bowling ball. Round to the nearest hundredth of a cubic inch.

ALGEBRA MADE EASY UNIT 21
Ratio, Rate & Proportion

The word **ratio** simply refers to an expression that is written in terms of the quotient of two quantities. Ratio can be expressed in either of three ways, for example the ratio of A to the ration of B is written as

I.   Ratio of A to B (written out)
II. A:B   (Colon notation)
III. A/B   (Quotient notation)

Example the ratio of 6 to 8 can be written as **6:8** or **6/8**.

When ratio is used to compare two different measurements it is classified as new term call **rate**. For example, the comparison between the number of miles that your car get to one gallon of gas is call the rate of the car given in miles per gallon. Example the Toyota Corolla is estimated to give 35 mpg.

We use the concept of rate to get answers to certain types of questions.

Example1: You have a car that has a capacity of 15 gallons and you were able to drive 570 miles before your car is empty. How much miles do you get to the gallon in your car.

Solution
The question is simply asking you to calculate the rate of the car which is given by 570/15 = 38.

   That means that the car is giving you 38 miles to the gallon or 38mpg.

When two pairs of numbers such as (3, 2) and (6, 4) have the same **ratio**, we say that they are **proportional**.

We use this relationship to help us solve some types of problems. For example 2/3 had the same ration as 4/6 therefore we say that the two expressions are proportional.

$$2/3 = 4/6$$

The process for solving equations using this principle is called cross products.
To solve x/a = c/d equate *cross products* and then divide on both sides to get *x* alone.

> That is **xd = ac** which gives $x = \dfrac{ac}{d}$

Example 2: solve x/8 = 6/5

Solution
5x = 6*8
x = 48/5
x = 9.6

Application

If you are mixing fruit punch and you have the concentrated mix that states to mix 4 ounces of the mixture with 8 ounces of water. If you have 36 ounces of water how much of the concentrated mix would you need?

Solution Let c represent the amount of mix that would be needed.

$$\frac{\text{Mix suggested}}{\text{Water suggested}} = \frac{\text{Mix Needed}}{\text{Water you have}}$$

$$\frac{4}{8} = \frac{c}{36}$$

$4*36 = 8c$

$\frac{4*36}{8} = c$; $c = 18$

That means that you would need 18 ounces of the concentrated mix.

Example 2: If you had a MS Word document that has a picture that had a width of 2 in. and a height 3 in. and you increased the width to 2.5 in. How much should the height be increased to keep the image proportionate?

Solution

$\frac{\text{Width}}{\text{Height}} = \frac{\text{New width}}{\text{New Height}}$; $\frac{2}{3} = \frac{2.5}{h}$; $h = \frac{2.5*3}{2}$; $h = 3.75$

To keep the image proportionate the height would need to be increased to 3.75 in.

Rate, Ratio & Proportion Exercise

Solve the following;

(1) For every 5 persons having a vehicle; 2 have cars, and 3 have SUV's or Trucks. What is the ratio of car owners to SUV's or Trucks owners?
(2) Find the ratio of 1.2 to 1.5 and then simplify.
(3) *Salary:* A student working at a community center for the summer earned $3762 for working 12 weeks. What was the rate per week?
(4) *Mileage*: A 2011 Nissan Altima can go 468 miles on 18 gallons of gasoline. What is the ratio of miles to gallons?
(5) $3/x = 9/15$
(6) $y/3 = 20/4$
(7) *Mixture:* If 5 ounces of a concentrated mix must be mixed with 8 ounces of water, how many ounces of concentrated mix would be mixed with 36 ounces of water?
(8) *Travel:* On a road atlas, 1 inch represents 24.5 miles. If two cities are 3.75 inches apart on the map, how far apart are they in reality?
(9) *Class Size*: Last year a summer camp had 195 students and they had 13 teachers. If they are planning for 255 students this year and what to keep the same student to teacher ratio how many teachers do the need to have?
(10) *Mixture:* A 40 pounds bag of fertilizer can cover 5000 square feet of lawn, what is the rate per square feet?

ALGEBRA MADE EASY UNIT 22
Percent & Application Of Percentage

Percentage is a way of expressing a number as a fraction of 100; that is it is a ratio of the number and 100. When we talk about percent we talking about representing a number as a fraction of 100 parts. This is usually indicated by the symbol "%". For example 47 percent of 100 is written as **47/100** or **47%**.

47/100 can also be written in **decimal form** as **0.47**

> **How this is Done**
> - To show that the number is less than 1 you put a 0 and then a point
> - Since you are dividing by 100 there needs to be 2 digits after the decimal point. So 47/100 becomes 0.47
> - If you had 4/100 that would be equal to 0.04
> - Take note of where the zero appeared, is important to satisfy the requirement that there be two digits after the decimal point.

When solving percentage problem it is best to first represent the percentage as a **decimal** and then translate the expression into an equation and then solve. Most percentage problem can be translated into an equation of the form **Amount = Percent number × Base**.

When translating use the following convention;
- "**Of**" translates to "*" or **multiplication**
- "**Is**" translates to "="
- "**What**" translates to a **variable**
- "**%**" translates to the **decimal equivalent**

Example 1: solve 23% of 25 is what?

<u>Solution</u>
First translate
What is 23% of 25?
  $a = 0.23 * 25$

Now you can easily solve for a by carrying out the operation.
$a = 5.75$

Example 2: What is 15% of 24?

<u>Solution</u>
First translate
What is 15% of 24?
  $a = 0.15 * 24$

Now you can easily solve for a by carrying out the operation.
  $a = 3.6$

Example 3: 65 is what percent of 150?

Solution
First translate
65 is what percent of 150?
$$65 = p * 150$$

Now you can easily solve for a by carrying out the operation.
$$p = 0.4333$$

Since you need to state your answer as percentage you need one additional step which is to multiply by 100 to get **43.33%**

Basic Forms of Percent Application
There are three basic situations that you can encounter when dealing with percent and those situations are mentioned below.
1. **Finding the *amount*** (the result that you get when you take the percentage)
   Example: What   is   25%   of   80?
   Translation: a   =   25%   ·   80
2. **Finding the *base*** (the number you are taking the percent of)
   Example: 25   is   25%   of   what number?
   Translation: 25   =   25%   ·   b
3. **Finding the *percent number*** (the percent of one number to the other)
   Example: 25   is   what percent   of   80?
   Translation: 25   =   p   ·   80

Percentage Increase or Decrease
Note that when you are talking about percentage increase or percentage decrease you must first find the amount of increase or decrease and then apply the concept.

Example 4: The cost of an oil change increased from $24.99 to $29.99 what is the percentage increase?

Solution
Original price = $24.99   New Price = $29.99
The increase is 29.99 – 24.9 = 5
The percentage increase is in relation to the original price therefore you need to find out
   5 = what percent of 24.99
Percentage = 5/24.99 = 0.20 (*this is the decimal form*)
The answer is 20%.
        (*Note the formula works however it had to be used correctly*)

Example 5: **Salary:** Maisy earned a salary of $54,000 last year and receives a 4% raise this year. What is her new salary for this year?

Solution
Translate. What is the current salary plus 4% of the current salary?
        x =   54,000   +   0.04 • 54,000

Solve.
$$x = 54{,}000 + .04(54{,}000)$$
$$= 54{,}000 + 2160$$
$$= 56{,}160$$

The new salary for this year is $56,160.

Sales Tax

Since the task of buying and selling is an integral part of our lifestyle you are not usually given the relationship because you are expected to know it.

Percentage is important in the United States because sales tax is charged on many items that are purchased and sales tax is a form of percentage calculation. Here are two relationships that you should always keep in mind.

Sales Tax = Sales Tax Rate × Purchase Price
Total price = Purchase Price + Sales Tax

Example 5:
Sales Tax The sales tax rate in Houston Texas is 8.25%. How much tax is charged on the purchase of 4 books at $15.95 each? What is the total price?

Solution
a) We first find the cost of the books.
   4 × $15.95 = $63.80
b) The sales tax on items costing $63.80 is
   Sales tax rate × Purchase price
   0.0825   × $63.80   = $5.26
c) The total price is given by the purchase price plus the sales tax:
   $63.80 + $5.26, or $69.06

The sales tax is $5.26 and the total price is $69.06.

Commission

When you work for a **salary**, you receive the same amount of money each week or month. When you work for **commission**, you are paid a percentage of the total sales that you complete.
   Commission = Commission rate × Sales

Commission Example 1
Salary: Jessica is a car sales person and works at a local car dealer for a sales commission of 8%. What did she earn from the sale of $73,230 worth of new car sales?

Solution
Commission = Commission rate × Sales
$$C = 8\% \times 73{,}230$$
$$C = 0.08 \times 73{,}230$$
$$C = 5858.40$$

The commission is $5858.40.

Percent Exercise

1. What is 21% of 45?
2. *Sale:* A laptop computer is listed for $585 however there is a one day sale going on which is 20% off. How much does the computer cost?

3. What percent of 115 is 65?

4. 35 is 60 percent of what number?

5. *Purchase*: Gifton purchased a tie for $25 however the tie originally cost $40 what percent discount did Gifton receive on the purchase?

6. *Sales Tax:* Nick purchased a Nook for $199.99 and a Sony Clock Radio for iPod for $59.99 at Best Buy. The sales tax rate in Houston Texas is 8.25%. How much is the tax? What is the total cost of the purchase?

7. *Sale Tax:* If the tax on your purchase is $65.80 how much was your total purchase before tax? The tax rate is 8.25%.

8. *Sale Tax:* The sales tax is $140 on the purchase of a new couch which cost $1750. What is the sales tax rate on the couch?

9. *Commission:* Nick earns a commission of $17,340 from selling a $289,000 home. What is his commission rate on that sale?

10. *Commission:* Tony is a car salesman and earns a commission of 6% on sales. One week his commission was $1890 what was his total sales for that week?

ALGEBRA MADE EASY UNIT 23
Understanding Interest

Comparing interest rates is essential if one is to become financially responsible. A small change in an interest rate can make a *large* difference in the cost of a loan or an investment.

Interests are computed using one of two methods. ***Simple Interest*** is a simplified way of computing interest and is mainly used by banks on money they pay out. ***Compound Interest*** in a method of computing interest when the period is short and the interest is computed frequently. This is used by banks on money that is owed to them. It is also use to calculate the interest on investments.

Simple Interest
Suppose you have $1000 into Certificate of Deposit (CD) account that pays a rate of 7% annually. The $1000 is called the **principal** and the **interest rate** is 7%. At the end of the one year in addition to the principal, you would also get back 7% of the principal which is 7% **of $1000, or 0.07 × $1000, or $70.00**.

The $70.00 is called the **interest**, or more precisely, the **simple interest**. It is, in effect the price that a financial institution pays for the use of the money over time.

> The **simple interest** I on the principal P, invested for t years at interest rate r, is given by
> $$I = P \cdot r \cdot t$$

Example 1: Find the simple interest on $1500 invested at 3.5% after 6 months. What is the balance of the investment after the 6 months?

Solution
P = 1500   r = 3.5% = 0.035   t = 6 months = ½ year
I = P • r • t;
I = 1500 • 0.035 • ½
I = 116.25
   The interest is $116.25 so at the end of 6 months the balance of the investment is $1616.25

Compound Interest
When interest is paid on *interest*, it is called **Compound Interest**. This is the type of interest usually paid on investments or loans.

Let's say that you have $1000 in a savings account at 7%. At the end of 1 year, the account will contain the original $1000 plus 7% of $1000. Thus, the total in the account after 1 year will be 107% of $1000, or 1.07 × $1000, or $1070.

Now, let's say that you left the total of $1070 in the account for another year. At the end of the second year, the account will contain $1070 plus 7% of $1070. (*Note that the new balance is the sum of the total that you had plus the interest that you received after the first year*).

The interest at the end of the second year is 107% of $1070, or 1.07 × $1070, or **$1144.90**.

This is what we mean when we say that **interest is compounded on interest.**

> As you can see the process of doing this type of calculation can become really involved so to calculate the amount A on the principal P, invested for t years at an interest rate r, computed n times is given by **A = P(1+r/n)^{nt}**. However, as long as n=1 then the formula can be simplified as **A = P(1+r)^t**.

Example 1: The Murrays invest $5000 in an account paying 8% compounded annually. Find the amount in the account after 3 ½ years.

Solution
The compounding is annually, so $n = 1$.
P = $5000
r = 0.08
t = 3 ½
A = 5000(1 + 0.08) ^{3½}
A = 5000*1.309 = 6545

The amount in the account at the end of the 3 ½ year is $6545.

Interest Exercises
1. What is the simple interest on $3500 invested at an interest rate of 8% for 1 year?
2. What is the simple interest on a principal of $4500 invested at an interest rate of 8% for ¼ year?
3. What is the simple interest on a principal of $1500 invested at an interest rate of 7% for 4 months?
4. Find the amount in an account if $3000 is invested at 5%, compounded annually for 2 years.
5. The Murrays invest $5000 in an account paying 8% compounded quarterly. Find the amount in the account after 3 ½ years.

6. *Credit Card:* After the holidays, Kyla has a balance of $3216.28 on a credit card with an annual percentage rate (APR) of 19.7%. She decides not to make additional purchases with this card until she has paid off the balance.
   a) Many credit cards require a minimum monthly payment of 2% of the balance. At this rate, what is Kyla's minimum payment on a balance of $3216.28? Round the answer to the nearest dollar.
   b) Find the amount of interest and the amount applied to reduce the principal in the minimum payment found in part (a).
   c) What is the new balance after the first month's payment?

7. *Mortgage:* The Railings recently purchased their first home. They borrowed $165,000 at 4½% for 30 years (360 payments). Their monthly payment (excluding insurance and taxes) is $700.
   a) How much of their first payment is interest and how much is applied to reduce the principal?
   b) If the Railings pay the entire 360 payments as schedule, how much interest will be paid on the loan over the life of the loan?

ALGEBRA MADE EASY UNIT 24
Graphing Liner Equations

In statistical analysis a great deal of time is spent looking at and interpreting data presented to us in some form of graph. Therefore, it is important that we learn how to create graphs and also how to interpret the information that is presented in graphs. There are several types of graphs however this unit focuses on the line graph. **Line graphs** are often used to show a change over time as well as to indicate patterns or trends.

To plot a graph you need points (something to plot) called ordered pairs and you need an axis to plot them on. In some case you will be given that data and all you have to do is plot it on the axis and in other cases you will first have to determine what to plot and then plot it.

An **axis** is a pair of perpendicular lines, one horizontal and one vertical, that forms the two dimensional plane on which to plot the points. This plane is called the *Cartesian Plane*.

An **Ordered Pair** is a **point** that consists of a x and a y component that gives the location where that point exists on the plane. A point is usually written in the form (x, y), where x gives the location in regards to the horizontal axis and y gives the location in regards to vertical axis. Look at the point as direction to a particular location.

The point **zero** $(0, 0)$ is the *point of origination* and is the starting point for determining the location of each point in the plane. All points start at the origin (*it is the base location*).

Look at a graph as a map that consists of points that you are either trying to get to or giving someone directions to from your location.

Example Plotting Point: Plot the point (2, 3)

Solution
- To plot the point (2, 3) we start at the origin.
- Move 2 units in the horizontal direction.
- The second number 3, is positive. We move 3 units in the vertical direction (up).
- Make a "dot" and label the point.

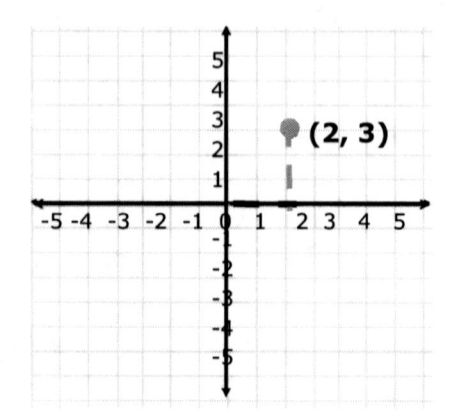

> *If someone gave you directions to the point you would go 2 miles east and then 3 miles north.*

Figure 1

Example Determining Point: Determine the coordinate of the point given.

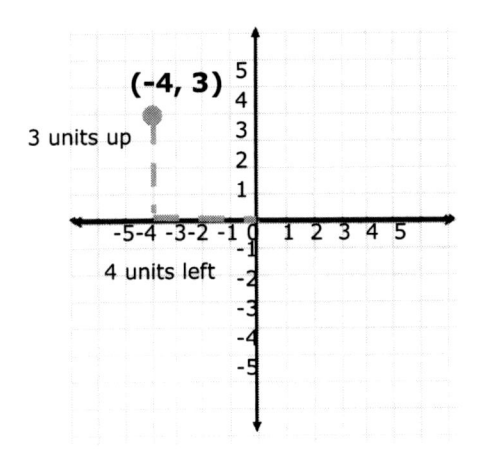

```
         (-4, 3)  5
                  4
3 units up        3
                  2
                  1
  -5-4 -3-2 -1  0  1 2 3 4 5
                 -1
  4 units left  -2
                 -3
                 -4
                 -5
```

> If you gave someone directions to the point you would tell them to go 4 miles west and then 3 miles north.

Figure 2

Note where the point is located then figure out how to get to it.
- Go 4 units to the left (-4)
- Go 3 units up (3)

Solution
The point is located at (-4, 3)

Drawing Graph
If you are given the data do the following;
- Draw the axis and put the scale on it *(that means to put numbers that are appropriate for the values given)*
- Then plot each point (pair of coordinate) on the axis.
- Finally connect the points.

Example 1: Every year, children die from heat stroke after being left unattended in a vehicle. The number of reported cases are given in the table below. Make a line graph of the data.

Year	Number of cases
1998	25
1999	31
2000	29
2001	35
2002	33
2003	42
2004	35

Source: Journal of the American Academy of Pediatrics

Solution
- Draw the axis and make sure that they are labeled evenly. (Put the Year on the *x*-axis and the number of cases on the *y*-axis.
- Take each pair and one by one find the location within the axis and put a point.
- Once all the pairs are accounted for connect the dots.

(The year is the fixed or independent number so it goes on the x-axis, and since the number of cases depends on the year it goes on the y-axis)

The result is shown in figure 3.

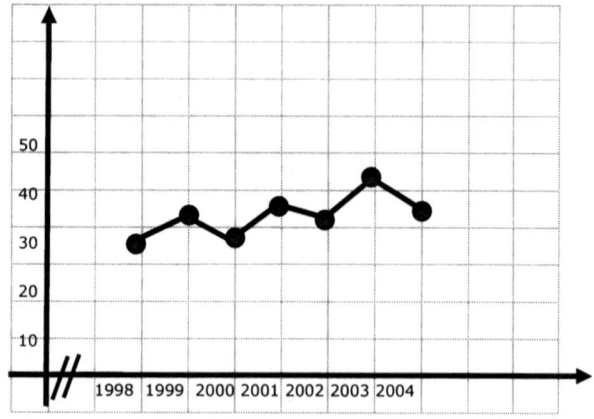

Figure 3

Note that the numbers on the y-axis is appropriate for the values of the number or cases. And the number on the x-axis represents the year. The break on the x-axis indicates that time started at year 0 which is not shown.

If you are not given the data set and is given a relationship (*that is an equation*) you need to find a set of data that matches the equation before you will be able to plot the graph. There are several methods to determine that data set; we are only going to cover two of those methods.

Method 1 – Find Ordered Pairs

Given an equation do the following:
- First pick at least three values for *x* (*pick any random numbers*)
- Then put each value for *x* into the equation that you are given to find the corresponding *y* value. That will give you three set of points (*ordered pairs*) to plot. (*note that you will have to solve for y three times*)
- Draw the axis and put the scale on it.
- Then plot each point on the same axis.
- Finally connect the points.

Example 1: Graph $y = -4x + 1$

<u>Solution</u>
- First pick 3 values for *x*; I picked -2, 0 and 2.
- Next use each of the values for x to find the corresponding value for *y*. That gives me 3 sets of points called ordered pairs.
 When $x = -2$; $y = -4(-2) + 1 = 9$
 When $x = 0$; $y = -4(0) + 1 = 1$
 When $x = 2$; $y = -4(2) + 1 = -7$

 The values are displayed below for clarity.

x	y	(x, y)
2	–7	(2, –7)
0	1	(0, 1)
–2	9	(–2, 9)

- Once you have found the ordered pairs then plot them on a pair of axis.
- Once you have plot all the points connect them. (*See figure 4*)

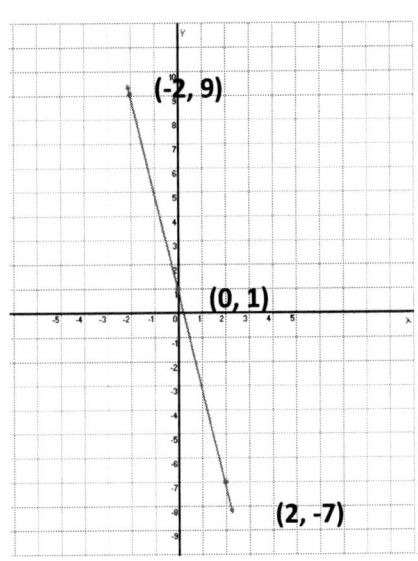

Figure 4

Intercepts

An *intercept* is a point that is common between two things. For example, there is a point of intercept between your drive way and the local road that allows you to come and go.

We are assuming that there is a point of commonality between the graph and the y-axis and also that there is a point of commonality between the graph and the x-axis. We are going to call the point of commonality with the y-axis the **y-intercept** given by **(0, b)** and call the point of commonality with the x-axis the **x-intercept** given by **(a, 0)**. Look at figure 5.

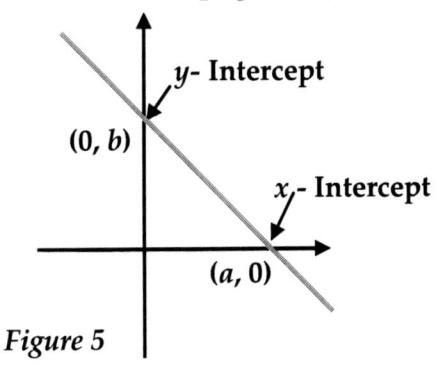

Figure 5

Note that for the y-intercept the value of $x = 0$ and for the x-intercept the value of $y = 0$. This is very important in finding intercepts.

- To find the **y-intercept** is (0, b). To find b, let $x = 0$ and solve the original equation for y.
- To find the **x-intercept** is (a, 0). To find a, let $y = 0$ and solve the original equation for x.

Example 2: Find the x and y intercepts of $2x - 4y = 8$

Solution
To find the x-intercept
Let $y = 0$, $2x - 4(0) = 8$
$2x = 8$
$x = 4$,   The x-intercept is (4, 0)

To find the y-intercept
Let $x = 0$, $2(0) - 4y = 8$
$-4y = 8$
$y = -2$,   The y-intercept is (0, -2)

Intercept Exercise
Find the x and y intercepts
1. $y = 4x - 6$
2. $y = 6x$
3. $y = ¼x + 3$

Method 2 – Using Intercept

In this method we are going to find (the *intercepts*) the points that are common between the graph that we are trying to draw and both of the axes.

> **Given an equation do the following;**
> - First find the **x-intercept**; *this is your first point to plot*. It is written as ***(what you calculated, 0)***
> - Then find the **y-intercept**; *this is your second point to plot*. It is written as ***(0, what you calculated)***
> - Then pick a value for x and find the corresponding y-value.
>   - That will give you three set of points (*ordered pairs*) to plot.
> - Draw the axis and put the scale on it.
> - Then plot each point on the axis.
> - Finally connect the points.

Example 3: graph $y = -4x + 1$

Solution
Let y be equal to 0, that gives
$0 = -4x + 1$
$-1 = -4x$
$x = ¼$ The point is (¼, 0)

Let x be equal to 0, that gives
$y = -4(0) + 1$
$y = 1$ The point is (0, 1)

Let x be equal to 1; that gives $y = -4(1) + 1$
$y = -4 + 1 = -3$
The point is (1, -3)

The graph is the same as *figure 4*; check the points.

You should practice and get proficient at drawing graphs. From this point forward whenever you are asked to draw a graph; draw the graph using the method that you are most proficient at.

Graph Exercise

Graph the following:
1. $4x - 3y = 12$
2. $2x + 3y = 6$
3. $x - 2y = 4$
4. $2x + y = 0$
5. $x = -1$
6. $x = 4$
7. $y = 3$
8. $y = -5$

Concept Application

1) *Shipping*: The cost c, in dollars, of shipping a FedEx Priority Overnight package weighing 1 lb or more a distance of 1001 to 1400 mi is given by **c = 2.8w + 21.05** where w is the package's weight in pounds.
   - Graph the equation and then use the graph to estimate the cost of shipping a 10 ½-pound package.

Solution at the end of this unit.

Solution to Concept Application

1) Select values for w and then calculate c; $c = 2.8w + 21.05$
   If $w = 2$, then $c = 2.8(2) + 21.05 = 26.65$
   If $w = 4$, then $c = 2.8(4) + 21.05 = 32.25$
   If $w = 8$, then $c = 2.8(8) + 21.05 = 43.45$

w	c
2	26.65
4	32.25
8	43.45

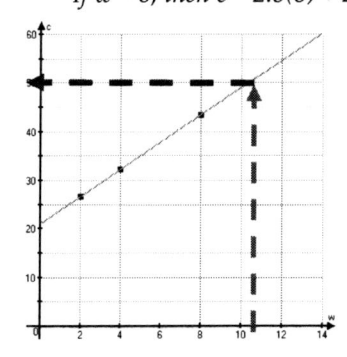

- To estimate the cost to mail a 10½ pound package, we locate the point on the line that is above 10 ½ and then find the value on the c-axis that corresponds to that point.
- The cost of shipping a 10½ pound package is about $50.50.

ALGEBRA MADE EASY – A Practical Approach to Algebra

ALGEBRA MADE EASY UNIT 25
Test 3

1) Find the area of the following objects
   (a) triangle with legs 4 in and 10 in
   (b) rectangle 6 ft wide
   (c) circle with diameter 12 ft

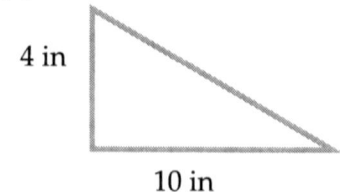

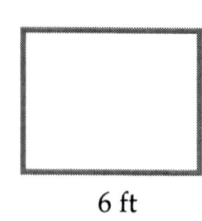

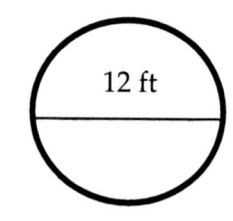

2) **Carpentry:** A board measures 6 ¾ feet and needs to be cut in five equal pieces. Find the length of each piece.

3) **Play Ground:** A football field is 300 feet long.
   (a) Write a formula that gives the length L of x football fields in feet.
   (b) The play ground is 870 feet. Use your formula to write an equation whose solution gives the number of football fields in 870 feet.
   (c) Solve your equation from part (b).

4) Given that $h(x) = x^2 - x$, find the values of
   (a) $h(-3)$ (b) $h(½)$ (c) $h(5k)$

5) Given $A = ½(h + b)$ solve for b

6) **Car Purchase:** George purchased a new car and paid $1750 in taxes. The tax rate is 7½%, what is the price of the car.

7) **Salary Increase:** Maisy got a 6% pay raise bringing her salary to $58,300. What was her salary before the raise?

8) **Height:** A stone is projected vertically upwards. Its height h in meters, after t seconds, is given approximately by the formula $h = 20t - 5t^2$. Use the formula to calculate its height after
   (a) 1 second   (b) 4 seconds

9) **Tuition:** A college tuition is currently $125 per credit. There are plans to raise tuition by 8% for next school year. What will the new tuition be per credit?

10) **Bank Loans:** Two bank loans, one for $5000 and the other for $3000, cost a total of $550 in interest for one year. The $5000 loan has an interest rate 3% lower than the interest rate for the $3000 loan. Find the interest rate for each loan.

ALGEBRA MADE EASY UNIT 26
Introduction To Polynomials

A **polynomial** is a mathematical expression constructed with variables and constants (*known as coefficients*) using only the operation of multiplication, addition and subtraction and non-negative integer (whole number) exponents. There are different classifications of polynomials for example there are polynomials of one terms called *monomials*, or two terms called *binomials* or three terms called *trinomials*. All other expression with four or more terms are simply referred to as *polynomials*.

Polynomials can have one variable or it can have more than one variable, we will focus on those with one variable.

These **are examples of** polynomials in one variable:

- x
- $4x + 5$
- $-8x^3 - (5/9)x + 6$
- 9

These are examples that are **not** polynomials

- $1/(x+3)$ is not, because division is not allowed
- $1/x$ is not because division is not allowed
- x^{-2} is not, because the exponent is "-2" (exponents can only be a whole number)
- $\sqrt{x}$ is not, because the exponent is "½" a fraction.

But these **are** allowed:

- **$x/2$ is allowed**, because it is also $(½)x$ (the coefficient is ½, or 0.5)
- also **$3x/8$** for the same reason (the coefficient is 3/8, or 0.375)
- $\sqrt{2}$ is allowed, because it is a constant (= 1.4142...etc)

A **monomial** is an expression of the type ax^n, where a is a real number constant and n is a nonnegative integer.
Examples of monomials are:
$3x^2$ 2 $2x$ $3x^6$ 0

A polynomial that has two terms is called a **binomial**.
Example of binomials are:
$2x + 1$ $y - 5$ $3x^2 - 2$

A polynomial that has three terms is called a **trinomial**.
Example of trinomials are:
$3x^2 + x - 2$ $x^2 - 2x + 1$

A **Variable** is an alphabetical letter that is use to represent the unknown. We typically use x and y however any number can be used as long as it is declared.

A **Coefficient** is a number that is use to be the multiplier of the variable. For example $3x$ means that x is multiplied by 3 and that makes 3 the coefficient.

Constant is a number that is usually on its own.

Exponents is the power to which the variable is raised.

A **Term** is either a number or a combination of a variable and a number. Terms are usually separated by either addition"+" or subtraction "-".

When **terms** have the same variable and the variable is raised to the same power, we say that they are **like terms**.

Degree
The **degree of a term** of a polynomial is the exponent of variable in that term. For example if you have $2x^2$ the degree is 2 because the exponent of x is 2.

The **degree of the polynomial** is the largest of the degrees of the terms.

Example 1: Identify the degree of the polynomial.
$2x^2 - 8x^3 + 4x^4 + 9x - 12$.

<u>Solution</u>
The largest exponent is 4.
The degree of the polynomial is 4.

When there are more than one variable in a term the exponent of each variable is added together to find the degree of the term. (*This is the only case when this is done*)

Example 2: Find the degree of $3a^5b$

<u>Solution</u>
The degree is 6 because you have a^5 and b^1 that makes the overall power of the term 6.

Standard Form
We usually arrange polynomials in **descending order** of the power of the variable; this is the standard form for representing a polynomial.

Arrange the polynomial in descending order.
$4x^6 + 8x^7 + 2x^2 + 3x^3 + x^4$

Solution
$4x^6 + 8x^7 + 2x^2 + 3x^3 + x^4 = 8x^7 + 4x^6 + x^4 + 3x^3 + 2x^2$

Introduction to Polynomial Exercise
Identify the coefficient of each term in the polynomial and state the degree of the polynomial.
1) $3x^4 - 8x^2 + 2x - 9$
2) $2x^2 - 4x^3 + 3$
3) $-3x^3 + x^2$

Concept Application
1) *Home Project*: Nick is building play house for his three children one child is 3ft 6 inches tall, another is 4ft 2 inches tall and the third child is 40 inches tall. How tall should the door to the play house be so that all three can enter standing upright?

Solution at the end of this unit.

Solution to Concept Application
1) 3ft 6 inches = 42 inches; 4ft 2 inches = 50 inches and the other child is 40 inches. To make the door so that everyone can enter upright the door needs to be at least 50 inches tall.

ALGEBRA MADE EASY UNIT 27
Adding & Subtracting Polynomials

In this unit we will start looking at operation on polynomials. We will start with the two most basic operations, addition and subtraction.

Adding Polynomials
When combining (adding) one polynomial to another polynomial combine each term that is similar by adding the coefficients of the terms. *Note that there are no operations on the variables; the variables only sever to let you know which terms are similar.*

Steps for Adding Polynomials
- Arrange the terms in columns
- Combine the like terms (*Add the coefficients*)

Example 1: Add $(-11x^3 + 7x^2 - 11x - 5)$ and $(16x^3 - 7x^2 + 3x - 15)$

Solution
$$-11x^3 + 7x^2 - 11x - 5$$
$$+\ 16x^3 - 7x^2 + 3x - 15$$
$$\overline{5x^3 + 4x^2 - 8x - 20}$$

Adding Polynomial Exercise
Add the following;
1) $2x + 5y$ and $3x - 2y$
2) $3x^2 + 4x - 2$ and $-7x^2 - 10x + 17$
3) $-6x^3 + 7x - 2$ and $5x^3 + 4x^2 + 3$
4) $3 - 4x + 2x^2$ and $-6 + 8x - 4x^2 + 2x^3$
5) $10x^5 - 3x^3 + 7x^2 + 4$ and $6x^4 - 8x^2 + 7$ and $4x^6 - 6x^5 + 2x^2 + 6$

Opposites of Polynomials
To find an equivalent polynomial or the **opposite** of a polynomial, change the sign of every term. This is the same as multiplying each term by –1.

Example 2: Simplify: $-(-8x^4 - x^3 + 9x^2 - 2x + 72)$

Solution
$$-(-8x^4 - x^3 + 9x^2 - 2x + 72)$$
$$= 8x^4 + x^3 - 9x^2 + 2x - 72$$

Opposite Exercise
Find the Opposite of the following;
$4x^5 - 6x^3 + 4x + 20$

Opposite Answer
$-4x^5 + 6x^3 - 4x - 20$

Subtracting Polynomials

To subtract two polynomials, change the sign of every term of the second polynomial (*find the opposite*). Then put both polynomials in columns and then add this result of the second polynomial to the first polynomial.

Steps for Subtracting Polynomials
- Find the opposite of the polynomial to be subtracted
- Arrange the terms in columns
- Combine the like terms (*Add the coefficients*)

Example 3: Subtract: $(6x^2 - 4x + 7) - (10x^2 - 6x - 4)$

Solution

$$\begin{aligned} 6x^2 &- 4x + 7 \\ -10x^2 &+ 6x + 4 \\ \hline -4x^2 &+ 2x + 11 \end{aligned}$$

Subtracting Polynomial Exercise
Subtract the following:
1) $(x^3 - x^2 + 2x - 12) - (-2x^3 - x^2 - 3x)$
2) $(9x^2 + 7x - 2) - (2x^2 - 4x - 6)$
3) $(8y^3 - 10y^2 - 14y - 2) - (5y^3 - 3y + 6)$
4) $(10x^5 + 2x^3 - 3x^2 + 5) - (-3x^5 + 2x^4 - 5x^3 - 4x^2)$
5) $(8x^5 + 2x^3 - 10x) - (4x^5 - 5x^3 + 6)$

Application

1) *Caloric Need*: The Harris-Benedict principle states that the number of calories needed each day by a moderately active woman who weights w pounds, is h feet tall, and is A years old can be estimated by the polynomial $655 + 4.3w + 4.7h - 47A$. Jamie is moderately active, weight 145 lbs is 5feet 8 inches cm tall and is 48 yrs old. What are her daily caloric needs?

2) *Caloric Need*: Harris-Benedict principle for males is given by the equation $66 + 6.3w + 12.9h - 6.8A$. Find the daily caloric needs for a man that is 200 lbs, 6feet 2 inches and is 35 yrs old.

3) *Lung Capacity*: The polynomial equation $C = 0.041h - 0.018A - 2.69$ can be used to estimate the lung capacity C in liters of a person of height h in centimeters and age A in years.
   1) Find the ling capacity of a 28 year old person who is 175 cm tall.

4) *Lung Capacity*: Find the ling capacity of a 28 year old person who is 175 cm tall.

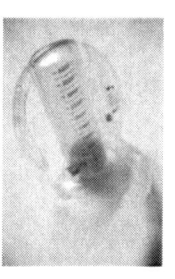

ALGEBRA MADE EASY UNIT 28
Multiplication Of Polynomials

We will continue looking at operation on polynomials. In this unit we will look at multiplying polynomials. The first concept that we are going to discuss is the use of the distributive property to eliminate the parenthesis.

Example 1: Simplify $4x^2(3x + 5)$

Solution
First use the distributive property to remove the parenthesis and it necessary combine any like terms.
$(3x)(4x^2) + (5)(4x^2)$
$12x^3 + 20x^2$

Remember that $(x^2)(x) = x^3$ because you add the indices.

> To find an equivalent expression for the product of two monomials involves two steps;
> 1. Multiply the coefficients
> 2. Then multiply the variables using the product rule for exponents.

Example 2: Find the product of $(4x)$ and $(3x^2)$

Solution
$(4*3)(x*x^2) = 12x^3$

Multiplying Monomial Exercise
Multiply the following:
1) $(6x)(7x)$
2) $(5a)(-a)$
3) $(-8x^6)(3x^4)$
4) x and $x + 7$
5) $6x(x^2 - 4x + 5)$

Multiplying a Monomial and a Polynomial

> To multiply a monomial and a polynomial, multiply each term of the polynomial by the monomial.

Example 3: Multiply: $5x^2(x^3 - 4x^2 + 3x - 5)$

Solution

$5x^2(x^3 - 4x^2 + 3x - 5)$
$= (5x^2)(x^3) - (5x^2)(4x^2) + (5x^2)(3x) - (5x^2)(5)$
$= 5x^5 - 20x^4 + 15x^3 - 25x^2$

Multiply Monomial and Polynomial Exercise
Multiply each of the following.
1) $x + 3$ and $x + 5$
2) $3x - 2$ and $x - 1$
3) $x + 8$ and $x + 5$
4) $x + 5$ and $x - 4$

Product of Two Polynomials

> To multiply two polynomials P and Q, select one of the polynomials, say P. Then multiply each term of P by every term of Q and collect like terms.
>
> If $P = (a + b)$ and $Q = (c + d)$
> $PQ = (a + b)(c + d) = ab + ad + bc + db$

We are going to use columns for clarity; think back to the time when you first learned to do long multiplication. Those are the steps that we will follow.

Example 4: Multiply: $(5x^3 + x^2 + 4x)(x^2 + 3x)$

Solution

$$\begin{array}{r} 5x^3 + x^2 + 4x \\ x^2 + 3x \\ \hline 15x^4 + 3x^3 + 12x^2 \\ 5x^5 + x^4 + 4x^3 \\ \hline 5x^5 + 16x^4 + 7x^3 + 12x^2 \end{array}$$

← First multiply by $3x$
← Next multiply by x^2
← Add the results

Example 5: Multiply: $(-3x^2 - 4)(2x^2 - 3x + 1)$

Solution

$$\begin{array}{r} 2x^2 - 3x + 1 \\ -3x^2 \quad\quad - 4 \\ \hline -8x^2 + 12x - 4 \\ -6x^4 + 9x^3 - 3x^2 \\ \hline -6x^4 + 9x^3 - 11x^2 + 12x - 4 \end{array}$$

← First multiply by -4
← Next multiply by $-3x^2$
← Add the results

This method works best when multiplying polynomials with 3 or more terms. Take a moment to practice.

Product of Two Polynomials Exercise
Multiply using columns;
1) $(x - 2)(3x + 7)$
2) $p^2 + 3p - 2$ by $p + 2$
3) $(5x^2 + 2)(x^3 - 4x^2 + 3x - 5)$
4) $(2z^3 - 3z^2 + 4)(-2z - 3)$
5) $(-3x^2 + 5x - 2)(-5x - 6)$

FOIL Method

The FOIL method is another method of multiplying polynomials. This method only works on polynomials that have two terms (*that is, on binomials*). To multiply two binomials, $A + B$ and $C + D$, multiply the First terms AC, the Outer terms AD, the Inner terms BC, and then the Last terms BD. Then combine like terms, if possible.

$$(A + B)(C + D) = AC + AD + BC + BD$$

Multiply **First** terms: AC.
Multiply **Outer** terms: AD.
Multiply **Inner** terms: BC.
Multiply **Last** terms: BD
↓
FOIL

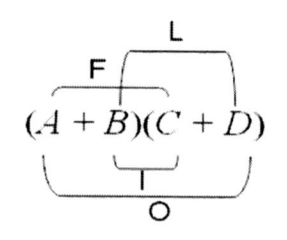

Let's look at an example together.

Example 6: Multiply: $(x + 4)(x^2 + 3)$

Solution

$$(x + 4)(x^2 + 3) = x^3 + 3x + 4x^2 + 12$$
$$= x^3 + 4x^2 + 3x + 12$$

Note that the terms are rearranged in descending order for the final answer.

FOIL Method Exercise
Multiply using the FOIL method
1) $(x + 8)(x + 5)$
2) $(y + 4)(y - 3)$
3) $(5t^3 + 4t)(2t^2 - 1)$
4) $(4 - 3x)(8 - 5x^3)$

Polynomial General Exercise
Multiply using the most appropriate method.
1) $(x + 8)(x + 5)$
2) $(y + 4)(y - 3)$
3) $(5t^3 + 4t)(2t^2 - 1)$
4) $(4 - 3x)(8 - 5x^3)$
5) $(3x^5 + 2x^2 + 3x)(2x^2 + 4x)$
6) $(x + 9)(x + 9)$
7) $3x^2(4x^2 + x - 2)$

Application

8) **Manufacturing:** The H&L Packing Company manufactures trash bags in three different sizes. The bags are rolled tightly together and then packed in a rectangular box. The length is 8 inches more than the width and the height is 1 inch more than the height.
   a) Write the polynomial that represents the general volume of the package.
   b) Find the dimensions for a box whose volume is 60in³ that holds small kitchen bags. And find the dimensions for a box whose volume is 240 in³ that holds tall kitchen bags.

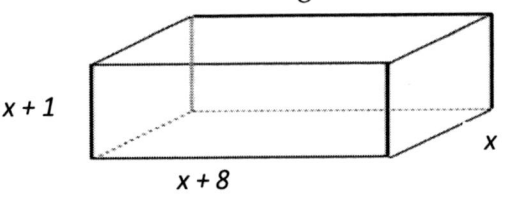

9) **Lawn Space:** Gifton decided to install a 8-ft by 8-ft shed in his back yard lawn area that measures x-ft by x-ft. Find a polynomial that represents the remaining area of the lawn that has grass.

ALGEBRA MADE EASY UNIT 29
Special Products

In this unit we are going to discuss **special products**. When we talk about special products we are simply referring to a *"short cut"* method to find the solutions to certain binomials that we encounter on a regular basis. For example, $(a + b)^2$ or $(a - b)^2$.

A common error that students often make is to think that $(a + b)^2$ is equal to $a^2 + b^2$. For example: $(x + 2)^2$ **IS NOT EQUAL to** $x^2 + 4$. The correct solution is $(x + 2)^2 = x^2 + 4x + 4$. I got this by writing out the expression $(x + 2)^2$ as $(x + 2)(x + 2)$ and then carry out the multiplication. You could also use the distribution method or the FOIL method which stands for **First, Outer, Inner, and Last** that you previously learned.

The special cases or *"short cut"* methods that we are referring to are called **the Sum & Difference of Perfect Squares and Difference of Two Squares Methods**. These formulas are derived from multiplying the polynomial out. However there is a pattern, which once recognized can be applied to get to the answer more quickly and hence the *"short cut"*. The important thing to keep in mind is that these *"short cut"* will only work with binomials.

Square of a Binomial (also known as the Perfect Square Method)
I. $(a + b)^2 = (a + b)(a + b)$
              $= a^2 + 2ab + b^2$

$$(A + B)^2 = A^2 + 2AB + B^2$$

II. $(a - b)^2 = (a - b)(a - b)$
              $= a^2 - 2ab + b^2$

$$(A - B)^2 = A^2 - 2AB + B^2$$

Since you have proven the formulas, whenever you identify the pattern in a problem you can simple use the formula instead of doing all the steps of the multiplication.

Example 1: Simplify $(3x + 4)^2$

Solution
- The first step is to determine which of the patterns this problem follows
 This problem has the same pattern as I.
- The next step is to determine *a* and *b*.
 a = 3x and b = 4
- Finally substitute for *a* and *b* and simplify.
 $(3x)^2 + 2(3x)(4) + (4)^2$
 $9x^2 + 24x + 16$

 Answer: $(3x + 4)^2 = 9x^2 + 24x + 16$

Example 2: simplify $(x - 2)^2$

Solution
- The first step is to determine which of the patterns this problem follows
  This problem has the same pattern as II.
- The next step is to determine *a* and *b*.
  a = x and b = 2 (Note that the minus is accommodated for in the formula to help to recognize the pattern)
- Finally substitute for *a* and *b* and simplify.
  $(x)^2 - 2(x)(2) + (2)^2$
  $x^2 - 4x + 4$
  Answer: $(x - 2)^2 = x^2 - 4x + 4$

Binomial Square Exercise
Multiply;
1) $(x + 8)^2$
2) $(3x + 5)^2$
3) c) $(y - 7)^2$
4) d) $(4x - 3x^5)^2$

The other "*short cut*" method for multiplying two polynomials is the **Difference of Squares** given by the formula $(a + b)(a - b) = a^2 - b^2$. This formula is also derived from multiplying out the expression.

$(a + b)(a - b) = a^2 + ab - ab + b^2$
$ = a^2 - b^2$

$$(A + B)(A - B) = A^2 - B^2$$

Just like before whenever you identify the pattern in a problem you can simple use the formula instead of doing all the steps of the multiplication.

Example 3: Multiply $(2x + 3)(2x - 3)$

Solution
- The first step is to determine whether or not the problem fits the pattern.
  This problem fits the pattern.
- The next step is to determine *a* and *b*.
  a = 2x and b = 3 (Note that the minus is accommodated for in the formula to help you identify the pattern)
- Finally substitute for *a* and *b* and simplify.
  $(2x)^2 - (3)^2 = 4x^2 - 9$
  Answer $(2x + 3)(2x - 3) = 4x^2 - 9$

Difference of Squares Exercise
Multiply;
1) $(x + 8)(x - 8)$
2) $(6 + 5w)(6 - 5w)$
3) $(4t^3 - 3)(4t^3 + 3)$

Tips for Multiplying Two Polynomials

- Is the multiplication the product of a monomial and a polynomial? If so, multiply each term of the polynomial by the monomial.

- Is it the product of the sum or difference of the same two terms? If so, use the pattern
  $(A + B)(A - B) = (A - B)^2$

- Is the product the square of a binomial? If so, use the pattern that applies
  $(A + B)^2 = A^2 + 2AB + B^2$, or
  $(A - B)^2 = A^2 - 2AB + B^2$

- If neither of the above applies use the FOIL method

- Is the multiplication the product of two polynomials other than those above? If so, multiply each term of one polynomial by every term of the other polynomial. Use columns if you desire.

Multiply Polynomial Exercise
Multiply;
1) $(x + 5)(x - 5)$
2) $(w - 7)(w + 4)$
3) $(x + 9)(x + 9)$
4) $3x^2(4x^2 + x - 2)$
5) $(p + 2)(p^2 + 3p - 2)$
6) $(2x + 1)^2$

Concept Application
Application of this concept is given in unit 30.

ALGEBRA MADE EASY UNIT 30
Division Of Polynomials

In this unit we will look at the concept of dividing polynomials. To divide a polynomial by a monomial you take it term by term to do the division; that is, you divide each term in the numerator by the denominator. You divide the coefficients first and then use the division rules for the exponents.

Dividing By Monomials

Step 1: Divide the coefficients
Step 2: And then use the quotient rule for exponents to divide the variables:

Example 1: Divide the following;

(a) $\dfrac{-20x^{12}}{10x^4}$ (b) $\dfrac{3x^4}{15x^4}$ (c) $\dfrac{9x^6y^5}{3xy^5}$

Solution
(a) $-20/10 \; x^{12-4} = -2x^8$
(b) $3/15 \; x^{4-4} = 1/5$
(c) $9/3 \; x^{6-1} y^{5-5} = 3x^5$

Example 2: Divide $(5t^8 + 5t^7 + 15) \div 5t$

<u>Solution</u>
$\dfrac{(5t^8 + 5t^7 + 15)}{5t} = \dfrac{5t^8}{5t} + \dfrac{5t^7}{5t} + \dfrac{15}{5t} = t^7 + t^6 + 3/t$

Divide Monomial Exercise
Divide each term of the polynomial by the monomial.
1) $x^3 - 6x^2 + 9x + 3 \div -3$
2) $2x^6 - 8x^3 + 12x^2 + 24x \div 2x$
3) $x^5 + 24x^4 - 12x^3$ by $6x$
4) $-8x^6 + 12x^4 - 4x^2 \div 4x^2$
5) $25x^9 - 7x^4 + 10x^3 \div 5x^3$
6) $18x^7y^6 - 6x^2y^3 + 60xy^2 \div 6xy^2$
7) $-9ab^2 - 6a^3b^3 \div -3ab^2$
8) $21a^5b^4 - 14a^3b^2 + 7a^2b \div -7a^2b$

Dividing by Binomial
Take a journey back in time to when you first learn about long division.

Example 3: 100 divided by 3

Solution

```
      33
3)100        ← Start by saying 3 divided by 1; I can't. Then add the next digit to 1 to get 10
  -9         ← 10 divided 3; the result is 3
   10        ← 3 times 3 = 9, so minus 9 from 10. Bring down the other 0 and that another 10
   -9        ← 3 into 10 goes 3 times
    1        ← 3 times 3 = 9, so minus 9 from 10. This leaves a remainder of 1
```
The solution is 33 with remainder 1

This is the process that we will use to divide any polynomial where the divisor has more than one term. Let's look at a few examples. Note what is unique about each and how it is handled.

Example 4: Divide $x^2 + 7x + 12$ by $x + 3$.

Solution

```
             x
x + 3 ) x² + 7x + 12
       -(x² + 3x)        ← Multiply x + 3 by x using the distributive law
             4x          ← Subtract by changing signs and adding
```

Now we "bring down" the next term.

```
           x + 4
x + 3) x² + 7x + 12
      -(x² + 3x)
           4x + 12
          -(4x + 12)     ← Multiply x + 3 by 4 using the distributive law
              0          ← Subtract by changing signs and adding
```
The solution is x + 4 remainder 0

(As with dividing numbers you are done when the denominator is 0 or you cannot go any further.)

Example 5: Divide $15x^2 - 22x + 14$ by $3x - 2$.

Solution

```
              5x – 4
3x – 2)15x² – 22x + 14
      -(15x² – 10x)       ← Multiply 3x - 2 by 5x using the distributive law
           -12x + 14      ← Subtract by changing signs and adding & bring down 14
          -(-12x + 18)    ← Multiply 3x - 2 by -4 using the distributive law
                 6        ← Subtract by changing signs and adding
```

(As with the division of numbers you are done when the number is smaller than the devisor.)

The answer is 5x – 4 with R6. Another way to write the answer is $\quad 5x - 4 + \dfrac{6}{2x - 2}$

> To perform a division when there are missing terms we will create a place holder for any the missing term; that will minimize errors.

Example 6: Divide $x^5 - 3x^4 - 4x^2 + 10x$ by $x - 3$.

Solution

$$\begin{array}{r} x^4 \qquad\qquad -4x - 2 \\ x-3\,\overline{)x^5 - 3x^4 + 0x^3 - 4x^2 + 10x + 0} \\ \underline{-(x^5 - 3x^4)} \qquad\qquad\qquad\qquad \\ 0x^3 - 4x^2 + 10x + 0 \\ \underline{-(-4x^2 + 12x)} \qquad\quad \\ -2x + 0 \\ \underline{-(-2x + 6)} \\ -6 \end{array}$$

←——— Substitute 0 for the terms that are missing

The answer is $x^4 - 4x - 2 - \dfrac{6}{x-3}$

Example 7: Divide $x^3 - 3x^2 + 3x + 2$ by $x^2 + 1$.

Solution
Begin by writing $x^2 + 1$ as $x^2 + 0x + 1$

$$\begin{array}{r} x - 3 \\ x^2 + 0x + 1\,\overline{)x^3 - 3x^2 + 3x + 2} \\ \underline{x^3 + 0x^2 + x} \qquad\quad \\ -3x^2 + 2x + 2 \\ \underline{-3x^2 + 0x - 3} \\ 2x + 5 \end{array}$$

The quotient is $x - 3$ with remainder $2x + 5$. This result can also be written as
$x - 3 + \dfrac{2x + 5}{x^2 + 1}$

Divide by Polynomial Exercise
Divide each term of the polynomial.
1) $(x^2 - 3x + 1) \div (x - 2)$
2) $(x^3 - x + 2) \div (x - 2)$
3) $(2x^3 + 3x^2 + 3x - 1) \div (2x + 1)$
4) $(x^4 - x^3 + x^2 - x + 1) \div (x^2 - 1)$
5) $(-3x^3 + 8x^2 + x) \div (3x + 4)$

Application of Polynomials

1) **Volume of a Box:** The volume V of a box is $2x^3 + 4x^2$, and the area of its bottom is $2x^2$. Find the height of the box in terms of x. Make a possible sketch of the box, and label the length of each side.

2) **Heart Rate:** An athlete starts running and continues for 10 seconds. The polynomial $t^2 + 60$ calculates the heart rate of the athlete in beats per minute t seconds after beginning the run, where $t \leq 10$.
    (a) What is the athlete's heart rate when the athlete first starts to run?
    (b) What is the athlete's heart rate after 10 seconds?
    (c) What happens to the athlete's

3) **Compound Interest:** If P dollars are deposited in an account that pays 6% annual interest, then the amount of money after 3 years is given by $P(1 + 0.06)^3$. Find this amount when $P = \$700$.

4) **Concert Tickets:** Tickets for a concert are sold for $20 each.
    (a) Write a polynomial that gives the revenue from selling t tickets.
    (b) Putting on the concert costs management $2000 to hire the band plus $2 for each ticket sold. What is the total cost of the concert if t tickets are sold?
    (c) Subtract the polynomial that you found in part (b) from the polynomial that you found in part (a). What does this polynomial represent?

5) **Height Reached by a Baseball:** A baseball is hit straight up. Its height h in feet above the ground after t seconds is given by $t(96 - 16t)$
    (a) Multiply this expression.
    (b) Evaluate both the expression in part (a) and the given expression for Interpret the result.

6) **Height Reached by a Golf Ball:** When a golf ball is hit into the air, its height in feet above the ground after t seconds is given by $t(88 - 16t)$.
    (a) Multiply this expression.
    (b) Evaluate the expression in part (a) for $t = 3$. Interpret the result.

7) **Alcohol Consumption:** In 2007, about 239 million people in the United States were age 14 or older. They consumed, on average, 2.31 gallons of alcohol per person. Use scientific notation to estimate the total number of gallons of alcohol consumed by this age group. (*Source:* Department of Health and Human Services.)

8) **Federal Debt:** In 1990, the federal debt held by the public was $2.19 trillion, and the population of the United States was 249 million. Use scientific notation to approximate the national debt per person. (*Source:* U.S. Department of the Treasury.)

9) **Solution Mix:** How many milliliters of a 3% cranberry juice concentrate should be added to 400 milliliters of a 6% raspberry juice concentrate to dilute it to a 5% cran-raspberry concentrate?

ALGEBRA MADE EASY UNIT 31
Test 4

Evaluate the following;
1) $-3x + 7$, when $x = 8$

Identify the polynomial as a monomial, binomial, trinomial, or none of these. Give its degree.
2) $-15x$

Identify the degree of each term and the degree of the polynomial.
3) $2x^5 - 6x^2 + 9 - 8x^3$

Perform the indicated operation and simplify your answer
4) $(3x + 4) + (6x + 2)$
5) $y^6 \cdot y^0$
6) $(8 + 3x^5 + 6x^4) + (6x^5 - 8x^4 - 3)$
7) $(9x^8 - 8x^5 + 5x^2 + 9) + (9x^7 + 2x^5 - 5x)$
8) $(4k - 5)(3k^3 - 2k^2 - 3k + 4)$
9) $10x^7(8x^3 + 5x^2)$

10) $\dfrac{(9x)^{13}}{(9x)^{13}}$

11) $(3/5 - 6x^4)(3/5 + 6x4)$
12) $(25x + 18xy - 21y) - (28x - 8xy - 24y)$
13) $(6 - 7x^3 + 5x^5 + 3x^4) + (6x^4 - 3x^3 + 8 + 8x^5)$

14) $9x^6 - 20x^5 + 8$
    $- (6x^6 - 3x^5 + 14)$

15) $(2x + 10)(x + 4)$

16) $\dfrac{16x^5 - 10x^2 - 8x}{2x}$

17) $\dfrac{30x^8 - 10x}{10}$

18) **Finance**: The national debt of a country is $69,840,000,000 and the population is 7,760,000. What is the debt per person?
19) **Lung Capacity**: The polynomial $0.041h - 0.018A - 2.69$ can be used to estimate the lung capacity, in liters, of a female with height h cm and age A years. Find the lung capacity of a 60-year-old woman who is 162 cm tall. Round to the nearest liter.
20) **Baseball**: During the first seconds, the height h in feet of a baseball after t seconds is given by $h = -16t^2 + 119t + 4.0$. Estimate the height of the ball after 4 seconds.

ALGEBRA MADE EASY UNIT 32
Introduction To Factoring

In the next five units we will discuss various methods of factoring. As you learn each method you will find that you prefer some methods over others and that will be OK. Keep in mind that factoring the expression is only one step in the overall process of obtaining the solution to some questions. The goal will be to find the factors as quickly as possible using the best approach that you determine. You should be familiar with factoring numbers; we will take that one step further and work with polynomials.

Polynomials are frequently used in applications to approximate data and for estimating things such as the changes in the weather, the forecasted sales of a new product, the forecasted growth of population, and estimation of potential profits.

To *factor* a number is to find numbers that can be multiplied to give that number. Example: The factors of 6 are 2 and 3 or 6 and 1.

Similarly, to *factor* a polynomial is to find equivalent polynomials (*expressions*) that can be multiplied to give the original polynomial. Factoring a polynomial is to express a polynomial as a product of two or more polynomials.

A number is called a prime number if the only numbers that divide it evenly are 1 and itself. Similarly, *prime* polynomials are polynomials that have no factors other than 1. Like prime numbers, they have only 1 and themselves as factors. A common error that students often make is to conclude that if they could not factor an expression then it is *prime*. You should only conclude that an expression is prime after you have tried to factoring using at least two processes and failed to find any factors.

There are several methods for factoring polynomials and we are going to look at about four of those methods and then we will look at some *"short cuts"* that we can unitize whenever appropriate.

Factoring is the opposite of multiplication so this is the part of algebra where you can check your answer. I recommend checking your answer each time that solve a factor problem.

Factoring uses the concepts of exponents as well as just about every other concept that you have learnt up to this point. This concept goes a lot into data manipulation and will really demonstrate your understanding of polynomials and working with exponents.

Concept Application
Application of this concept is given in unit 37.

ALGEBRA MADE EASY UNIT 33
Greatest Common Factor

The first concept that we will look at is finding the **Greatest Common factor** (GCF). Recall that the **GCF** or the **Greatest Common Factor** is largest number that is common to all the terms in the expression.

Greatest Common factor of Numbers
- Find the largest number that divides evenly into all the coefficients of the terms.

Example
The numbers 20 and 30 have several factors in common, among them 2 and 5. The greatest of these common factors is called the **greatest common factor, GCF**. One way to find the GCF is by making a list of the factors of each number.

- The factors of 20: 1, 2, 4, 5, 10, and 20
- The factors of 30: 1, 2, 3, 5, 6, 10, 15, and 30
- Common numbers: 1, 2, 5, and 10.
- The GCF is 10.

For example if you are given the expression **21, -18, 45**. The GCF would be **3** since **3** is the largest term that could evenly divide all the terms.

Similarly, if you are given a polynomial you can factor the expression by finding the GCF. Let's look at an example together.

Greatest Common Factor of Polynomials

- Find the largest number that divides evenly into all the coefficients of the terms.
- The variable part of the greatest common factor always contains the smallest power of a variable that appears in all terms of the polynomial.

Example
Find the GCF of $30x^3$, $-48x^4$, $54x^5$, and $12x^2$.

Solution
Begin by finding the prime factor of each number.
$30x^3 = 2*3*5* x^3$
$-48x^4 = -1*2*2*2*2*3* x^4$
$54x^5 = 2*3*3*3* x^5$
$12x^2 = 2*2*3* x^2$

The GCF of the coefficients 30, -18, 54 and 12 is 6.
The GCF of these monomials x^3, x^4, x^5 and x^2 is x^2, because 2 is the smallest exponent of all the x's.

> **GCF of Polynomial**
> 1. Find the prime factorization of the coefficients, including –1 as a factor if any coefficient is negative.
> 2. Determine any common prime factors of the coefficients. For each one that occurs, include it as a factor of the GCF. If none occurs, use 1 as a factor.
> 3. Examine each of the variables as factors. If any appear as a factor of all the monomials, include it as a factor, using the smallest exponent of the variable. If none occurs in all the monomials, use 1 as a factor.
> 4. The GCF is the product of the results of steps (2) and (3).

Example Factor $4x^2 + 2x - 12$

Solution
Find the GCF for all the terms; I see **2**
Factor it out **2(   )**
Now divide each of the term by the GCF and put the result inside the parenthesis.
  $2(2x^2 + x - 6)$

Note that you are using the concept of division of polynomials that you learned a few units back.

Note that you do not throw the two away you put it on the outside of the parenthesis and then put the result of the division inside the parenthesis.

This is also look at as being the reverse for the Distribution Property.

To factor a polynomial with two or more terms of the form $ab + ac$, we use the distributive property with the sides of the equation switched: $ab + ac = a(b + c)$.

Multiply	Factor
$4x(x^2 + 3x - 4)$	$4x^3 + 12x^2 - 16x$
$= 4x \cdot x^2 + 4x \cdot 3x - 4x \cdot 4$	$= 4x \cdot x^2 + 4x \cdot 3x - 4x \cdot 4$
$= 4x^3 + 12x^2 - 16x$	$= 4x(x^2 + 3x - 4)$

> **Tips for Factoring**
> - Before doing any work, first determine the greatest common factor of all terms in the polynomial.
> - Use the distributive property to factor out the GCF if one exists.
>   - Find the GCF of the coefficients and then
>   - Find the GCF of the variable
> - Express each term as the product of the GCF and its other factor. That is **GCF(what is left)**

Example: Factor $12x^2 - 6x$

Solution
The GCF of 12 and 6 is 6
The GCF of x and x^2 is x.
The GCF is $6x$ so the result is **$6x(2x - 1)$**

GCF Exercise

Factor the following

1) $9a - 21$
2) $28x^6 + 32x^3$
3) $12x^5 - 21x^4 + 24x^3$
4) $9a^3b^4 + 18a^2b^3$
5) $-4xy + 8xw - 12x$

6) **Flight of a Golf Ball:** If a golf ball is hit upward at 66 feet per second (45 miles per hour), then its height in feet after t seconds is approximated by $66t - 16t^2$.
   a. Identify the greatest common factor.
   b. Factor this expression.

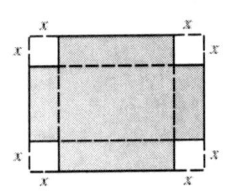

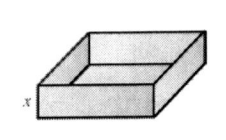

7) **Volume of a Box:** A box is constructed by cutting out square corners of a rectangular piece of cardboard and folding the sides. If the cutout corners have sides with length x, then the volume of the box is given by the polynomial $4x^3 - 60x^2 + 200x$

   a) Find the volume of the box when $x = 3$ inches.
   b) Factor out the greatest common factor for this expression.

ALGEBRA MADE EASY UNIT 34
Factoring By Grouping

In this unit we will look at a strategy for factoring polynomials that are four terms. The method that we will look at is called *Grouping*. In this strategy we will be looking to form groups of two terms with each term in the group having something in common. (*I call it the buddy system.*) Since you are starting with four terms there will usually be two groups of two's.

You will first find the GCF of each group of two's which will produce two new terms. Then find the GCF of the remaining two terms. Let's look at the steps and then look at how they are applied.

Steps to Factor by Grouping
- Group terms that have a common factor. (*Sometimes the terms must be rearranged.*)
- Factor out the common monomial factor from each group.
- Factor out the remaining binomial factor (if one exists).

Example Factor the following by grouping.
a) $3x^3 + 9x^2 + x + 3$
b) $9x^4 + 6x - 27x^3 - 18$

Solution

a) $3x^3 + 9x^2 + x + 3 = (3x^3 + 9x^2) + (x + 3)$ (*use parenthesis to form the groups*)
         GCF = $3x^2$ GCF = 1   (*find the GCF of each group*)
           = $3x^2(x + 3) + 1(x + 3)$
         GCF = $(x + 3)$ (*find the GCF of the new group*)
           = $(3x^2 + 1)(x + 3)$

b) $9x^4 + 6x - 27x^3 - 18$
     = $(9x^4 + 6x) + (-27x^3 - 18)$ (*use parenthesis to form the groups*)
    GCF = $3x$ GCF = -9   (*find the GCF of each group*)
     = $3x(3x^3 + 2) + (-9)(3x^3 + 2)$
     = $(3x - 9)(3x^3 + 2)$
GCF = $(3x^3 + 2)$ (*find the GCF of the new group*)
     = $3(x - 3)(3x^3 + 2)$

In essence you are finding the GCF (*in this case twice*) until there is no more GCF to be found.

Factor by Grouping Exercise
1) $xy + 3x - 5y - 15$
2) $x^4 - x^3 + 2x - 2$
3) $20x^4 - 25x^2 + 12x^2 - 15$
4) $2x^2 + 6xy + 4xy + 12y^2$

Take some time to practice this concept because you will use it later in other concepts.

ALGEBRA MADE EASY UNIT 35
Factoring By Trial And Error

There are two different kinds of polynomials. There are those where the leading coefficient is one *(i.e. the coefficient of the x^2 term is 1)* and there are those where the leading coefficient is something other than one. In this unit we will concentrate on factoring a polynomial of three terms *(a trinomial)* where the leading coefficient is one.

First let's list the steps and then look at some examples.

The Trial & Error Method
1. Enter x as the first term of each factor.
2. List all pairs of factors of the constant that adds up to the coefficient of the middle term.
3. Try various combinations to obtain the value for b in bx.

This is also called the reverse of the FOIL Method.

Example: Factor $x^2 + 2x - 8$.

Solution
Step 1: This is a trinomial with a leading coefficient of one. Start off by putting ( ) ( ) *remember that we are looking for something*something.* Think of the FOIL method in reverse.
Since the only way to get x^2 when you multiply is to have $x*x$ you can go ahead and put the x's in place.
$(x\ \ )(x\ \ )$

Step 2: To factor such a polynomial, we need to find to numbers that will give us a **product** of the third term (-8) and will also give us a **sum** of the middle term (2). Use the chart below for clarity.

Pairs of Factors for -8	Sum of factors
1, -8	-7
-1, 8	7
2, -4	-2
-2, 4	② ←

The value in the circle is the value of the middle term so the factors that you need are **-2 and 4**.
Let's check them.
1. 4 times -2 = -8 and
2. 4 + -2 = 2.

Step 3: Once you find the numbers put them in the parenthesis and check your result by multiplying to see if you end up with the original trinomial.
So the trinomial factors into **(x + 4)(x - 2)**.
$x^2 + 4x - 2x - 8 = x^2 + 2x - 8$ *checks*

Example 2 Factor: $x^2 + 7x + 12$

Solution
Step 1: $(x +)(x +)$
Step 2: We need a constant term that has a product of 12 and a sum of 7. We list pairs of numbers that multiply to give 12.

See the chart shown.

Step 3: Since $3 \cdot 4 = 12$ and $3 + 4 = 7$,
The factorization of $x^2 + 7x + 12$ is $(x + 3)(x + 4)$

To check we simply multiply the two binomials.
Check: $(x + 3)(x + 4) = x^2 + 4x + 3x + 12$
$= x^2 + 7x + 12$ *checks*

Pairs of Factors for 12	Sums of Factors
1, 12	13
2, 6	8
3, 4	⑦
−1, −12	−13
−2, −6	−8
−3, −4	−7

Trial & Error Exercise 1
1) $x^2 + 5x + 6$
2) $x^2 - 6x + 8$
3) $x^2 + 3x - 10$
4) $y^2 - 6y - 27$
5) $t^2 - 32 + 4t$

Since the trial and error method can get lengthy let's look at some situations where you can apply what you already know to reduce the number of trials.

Factor when "c" is positive
To Factor $x^2 + bx + c$ *when c* is positive use what you know about working with real numbers to reduce the number of trials that you do.

When the constant term of a trinomial is positive; look for two numbers with the same sign that is the same as the sign is that of the middle term.

$x^2 - 7x + 10\ (x - 2)(x - 5);$ (neg. + neg. = neg. and neg. • neg. = pos.)
$x^2 + 7x + 10\ (x + 2)(x + 5);$ (pos. + pos. = pos. and pos. • pos. = pos.)

Example 3: Factor: $y^2 - 8y + 15$

Solution
Since the constant term is positive and the coefficient of the middle term is negative, we look for the factorization of 15 in which both factors are negative. Their sum must be −8.
Let's look at the logic
- The factors of 15 are -3*-5, 3*5, -1*-15 and 1*15
- The middle term is negative so we are looking for the negative factors that will add up to -8.
- That means that the factors that we need are -3 and -5

The solution is $y^2 - 8y + 15 = (y - 3)(y - 5)$

Positive "c" Exercise
Factor each trinomial
1) $x^2 - 7x + 10$
2) $x^2 - 8x + 15$
3) $y^2 - 9y + 18$

Factor when "c" is negative

To Factor $x^2 + bx + c$ *when c is negative* use what you know about working with real numbers to reduce the number of trials that you do.

When the constant term of a trinomial is negative; look for two numbers whose product is negative. One must be positive and the other negative:

$x^2 + 4x - 21 = (x - 3)(x + 7)$ (neg. + pos. = pos*. and neg. • pos. = neg.)
$x^2 - 4x - 21 = (x + 3)(x - 7)$ (pos. + neg. = neg*. and pos. • neg. = neg.)

Select the two numbers so that the number with the larger absolute value has the same sign as *b*, the coefficient of the middle term.

Note the condition stated is specific to the problem given. See the Rules of Operation for the complete rules for subtracting negative numbers.

Example 4 Factor $x^2 - 5x - 24$

Solution
The constant term must be expressed as the product of a negative number and a positive number.

Let's look at the logic
- The factors of -24 are listed in the table shown.
- Since the sum of the two numbers must be negative, the negative number must have the greater absolute value.
- That means that the factors that we need are 3 and -8.

The solution is $x^2 - 5x - 24 = (x + 3)(x - 8)$

Pairs of Factors for 24	Sums of Factors
1, −24	−23
2, −12	−10
3, −8	(−5)
4, −6	−2
6, −4	2
8, −3	5

Negative "c" Exercise
Factor each trinomial
4) $x^2 - 3x - 4$
5) $x^2 + 7x - 8$
6) $t^2 - 2t - 24$

Prime Polynomials
- A polynomial that cannot be factored is considered to be **prime**.
  - Example: $x^2 - x + 7$
- Often factoring requires two or more steps. Remember, when told to factor, we should *factor completely*. This means the final factorization should contain only prime polynomials.

(CAUTION: Do not simple assume that if you cannot factor the expression it is prime; make sure to try more than one method of factoring before you draw that conclusion)

Key Points

To Factor $x^2 + bx + c$
1. First arrange in descending order.
2. Use a trial-and-error process that looks for factors of c whose sum is b.
3. If c is positive, its factors will have the same sign as b.
4. If c is negative, one factor will be positive and the other will be negative. If the sum of the two factors is the opposite of b, changing the sign of each factor will give the desired factors whose sum is b.
5. Check by multiplying.

Factoring when the coefficient of x^2 is not = 1
Let's look at what happens when the coefficient of the x^2 term is not one.
Example 5: Factor: $14x + 5 - 3x^2$

Solution
It is an important problem-solving strategy to find a way to make problems look like problems we already know how to solve. Rewrite the equation in descending order.
$$14x + 5 - 3x^2 = -3x^2 + 14x + 5$$
Step 1: Factor out the -1:
$$-3x^2 + 14x + 5 = -1(3x^2 - 14x - 5)$$
$$= -1(3x + 1)(x - 5)$$
The factorization of $14x + 5 - 3x^2$ is $-1(3x + 1)(x - 5)$.

Example 6: Factor: $6x^2 - xy - 12y^2$

Solution
No common factors exist; we examine the first term, $6x^2$ and note that there are two possibilities:
$$(2x + \;)(3x + \;) \quad \text{or} \quad (6x + \;)(x + \;).$$

The last term $-12y^2$, has the following pairs of factors:

$\quad\quad$ $12y * -y$ $\quad$ or $\quad$ $6y * -2y$ $\quad$ or $\quad$ $4y * -3y$
and $\quad$ $-12y*y$ $\quad$ or $\quad$ $-6y* 2y$ $\quad\quad$ or $\quad$ $-4y* 3y$

As you can see there are two possible pairs and six factors of $-12y^2$ which make the number of trials cumbersome. Since there is a 6 you cannot simply take the sum because the 6 plays a role. Instead you will need to take each pair of factor and try each of the factors until you get the right answer (that is the reason why it is called *trial and error*). You have to do multiple trials therefore you should expect some will not work out.

Trial   *Product*

$(2x - 6y)(3x + 2y)$ $6x^2 + 4xy - 18xy - 12y^2$
                            $= 6x^2 - 14xy - 12y^2$ **Not correct**

$(6x + 4y)(x - 3y)$ $6x^2 + 6xy - 4xy - 12y^2$
                            $= 6x^2 + 2xy - 12y^2$ **Not correct**

$(2x + 3y)(3x - 4y)$ $6x^2 - 8xy + 9xy - 12y^2$
                            $= 6x^2 + xy - 12y^2$ **Not correct**, *but only because of the sign of the middle term. So to correctly factor, we simply change the signs in the binomials.*

$(2x - 3y)(3x + 4y)$ $6x^2 + 8xy - 9xy - 12y^2$
                            $= 6x^2 - xy - 12y^2$ **Correct**

The correct factorization is **$(2x - 3y)(3x + 4y)$**.

As you can see when the coefficient of x^2 is not equal to 1 the trial and error method can become cumbersome and confusing. To simplify the process another method will be introduced in the next unit.

Trial & Error Exercise 2
1) $5x^2 - 10x - 40$
2) $2x^2 + 8x - 10$
3) $2t^3 - 6t^2 + 8t$

Concept Application
Application of this concept is given in unit 37.

ALGEBRA MADE EASY UNIT 36
Factoring – AC Method

In this unit we will look at another method of factoring trinomials. This method is called the **AC method**. It is so named because it uses the coefficient of x^2 the "**a**" and the constant "**c**" in the trinomial that is being factored. This method is used when the coefficient of x^2 is not one and the trial and error process is cumbersome.

Reminder: The standard form of a trinomial is $Ax^2 + Bx + C$

First let's list the steps and then look at some examples.

The AC-Method
1. Factor out the largest common factor, if one exists. Note that the GCF could be 1 or -1
2. Multiply the leading coefficient A and the constant C.
3. Try to factor the product AC so that the sum of the factors is B.
4. Split the middle term. That is, write it as a sum or difference using the factors found in step (3).
5. Factor by grouping.
6. Check by multiplying.

Example 1: Factor $8x^2 + 8x - 6$

Solution
Step 1: $2(4x^2 + 4x - 3)$ *factor out and GCF if one exist*
Step 2: $4 \bullet -3 = -12$ *multiply the leading coefficient A and C*
Step 3: The factors that we are looking for are -2 and 6 $(4 = 6 - 2)$
Step 4: Re-write $4x$ as $6x - 2x$
Step 5: $2(4x^2 - 2x + 6x - 3)$ *focus only on what is inside the big parenthesis*
    Factor by grouping $2(2x - 1)(2x + 3)$ *what is inside the big parenthesis*
Step 6: Check $2(4x^2 + 6x - 2x - 3) = 2(4x^2 + 4x - 3) = 8x^2 + 8x - 6$

Example 2: Factor $6x^2 - 19x + 10$

Solution
Step 1: Note that there is no common factor other than 1.
Step 2: Multiply the leading coefficient, 6 and the constant, 10: $(6)(10) = 60$.
Step 3: Find the factors of 60 in which the sum of the factors is the coefficient of the middle term, -19.
    $-15 * -4 = 60$ and $-15 + -4 = -19$.
Step 4: Express the middle term as a sum or difference using the factors found in step 3.
    $-19x = -15x - 4x$.
Step 5: Now there are four terms so factor by grouping as follows:
$$6x^2 - 19x + 10 = 6x^2 - 15x - 4x + 10$$
$$= 3x(2x - 5) - 2(2x - 5)$$
$$= (3x - 2)(2x - 5)$$
Step 6: Check: $(3x - 2)(2x - 5) = 6x^2 - 15x - 4x + 10$

$$= 6x^2 - 19x + 10$$

The factorization of $6x^2 - 19x + 10$ is **(3x – 2)(2x - 5)**

AC-Method Exercise

Factor using the AC method
1) $8x^3 + 10x^2 - 12x$
2) $5x^2 + x - 18$
3) $2x^2 + 7x - 4$
4) $3y^2 + 10y + 3$
5) $5m^2 - 11m + 2$

Concept Application

Application of this concept is given in unit 37.

ALGEBRA MADE EASY UNIT 37
General Factoring Strategies

When working with polynomials the key is to first look at what you have and then determine which tool (*that is which process*) to pull out and when. Keep in mind that it does not matter where you acquired the tool. (*Refer to the toolbox approach mentioned in the introduction*)

Here are some tips to consider when factoring.
  a. Always look for the greatest common factor (GCF) first. If there is one, factor out the largest common factor. (*Keep in mind that the GCF could be -1*)
  b. Check to make sure that the coefficient of the term in x^2 is positive, if not factor out -1 or multiply the entire expression or equation by -1.
  c. Then look at the number of terms.
     - **Two terms**: If you have two terms check to see
        - If you have a difference of squares and factor accordingly using the shortcut.
          $A^2 - B^2 = (A - B)(A + B)$.
        - If you have the *difference* of two cubes and factor accordingly.
          $A^3 - B^3 = (A - B)(A^2 + AB + B^2)$.
        - If you have the *sum* of two cubes and factor accordingly.
          $A^3 + B^3 = (A + B)(A^2 - AB + B^2)$.
     - **Three terms**: If the trinomial is a perfect-square trinomial, factor accordingly:
        - $A^2 + 2AB + B^2 = (A + B)^2$ or
        - $A^2 - 2AB + B^2 = (A - B)^2$.
        - If it is not a perfect-square trinomial, try using Trial & Error or the AC-Method.
     - **Four terms**: Try factoring by grouping.
  d. Always *factor completely*. If a factor with more than one term can still be factored, you should factor it. When no factor can be factored further, you are finished.
  e. Finally, always check your answer by multiplying to see if you get back what you started with.

Note that there are some problems that can be factored using more than one process this helps you to determine the best approach to use.

Example: Determine which method is the best to be use in each case and then solve the problem.
a) $x^2 + 10x + 25$
b) $z^3 + 8$

Solution
a) You have three terms so you should look to see if the expression fits into the criteria of the perfect-square trinomial. $x^2 + 10x + 25$ can be written as $x^2 + 10x + 5^2$; which is $x^2 + 2(5)x + 5^2$ so it fits the criteria and the shortcut process can be used. ***The solution is thus $(x + 5)^2$.***

b) You have two terms and one is a cube so the first step is to determine whether or not the second term can be written as a cube; if it can check to see if it fits the criteria then you can use the shortcut process. Given $z^3 + 8$; 8 can be written as 2^3 so the formula $A^3 + B^3 = (A + B)(A^2 - AB + B^2)$ can be use to solve the problem. $z^3 + 8 = z^3 + 2^3 = (z + 2)(z^2 - 2z + 2^2) = (z + 2)(z^2 - 2z + 4)$

As you saw being able to use the short cut process allowed us to arrive at the answer very quickly.

> **Keep in mind that factoring the expression is only one step in the overall process of obtaining the solution to some questions. We will be using this concept in the units to come. The goal is to be able to factor an expression quickly whenever the need arises.**

General Factoring Strategy Exercise
Find the best approach and factor each of the following
1. $25t^4 - 625$
2. $2x^3 + 14x^2 + 3x + 21$
3. $-x^5 - 2x^4 + 24x^3$
4. $x^2 - 18x + 81$
5. $12x^2y^3 + 20x^3y^4 + 4x^2y^5$
6. $ab + ac + wb + wc$
7. $36x^2 + 36xy + 9y^2$
8. $a^8 - 16b^4$

Concept Application

1) *Driving:* When you try to stop a car, the greater the speed the greater is the stopping distance. In fact, if you drive twice as fast, the braking distance will be about four times as much. And if you drive three times faster, the braking distance will be about nine times as much.
   a) If the braking distance D in feet required to stop a car traveling at x miles per hour on dry, level pavement can be approximated by $D = (1/11)x^2$. Calculate the braking distance for a car traveling 75 miles per hour.

2) *Communication:* Time Warner has a local cable tower. The guy wire on the tower is 3m less than the distance of the tower to the point where the wire is anchored. The area of the space formed between the guy wire and the tower is 35m². How tall is the tower and how far is the guy wire anchored from the tower?

Solutions at the end of this unit.

Solutions to Concept Application
1) $D = (1/11)75^2 = 511.36$. The breaking distance for the car is 511.36 ft.
2) $h = b - 3$; $A = 35$; $A = \frac{1}{2}bh$
   $35 = \frac{1}{2}b(b-3)$; $70 = b(b-3)$; $70 = b^2 - 3b$; $b^2 - 3b - 70 = 0$; $(b-10)(b+7) = 0$
   $b = 10$

The tower is 7 m tall and the guy wire is anchored 10 m from the tower.

ALGEBRA MADE EASY UNIT 38
Zero Property

A *quadratic equation* is simply an equation that is made of a polynomial of degree two. So far none of the methods that you have learned for solving equations will work for a polynomial.

Now that you have learned to factor expression let's look at how that is used to actually solve equations. This method is used for solving **quadratic equations**. Recall that a quadratic equation is one that has a term in x squared.

An equation $ab = 0$ is true if and only if $a = 0$ is true or $b = 0$ is true, or both are true. (A product is 0 if and only if one or both of the factors is 0.) That is, to get zero as the answer when you multiply, one or both of the things that are multiplied must be equal to zero. Recall that $A * 0 = 0$, for any real number.

Knowing this can help to solve equations that is equal to zero, that is called the **Zero Property**. To apply the zero property we will also utilize some of the other concepts that we have studied like factoring.

> **The Zero Property** requires that your equation be in the form
> $$(something) * (something) = 0$$
> If it is not, then you must first put it in that form before you can apply the zero property.
>
> *Note: you will not be told to factor however you were not given (something)(something) you need to recognize that the only way to get (something)(something) is to factor the expression.*

Example 1: Solve: $(x + 4)(x - 3) = 0$

Solution
In order for a product to be 0, at least one factor must be 0. Therefore, either
$$x + 4 = 0 \quad \text{or} \quad x - 3 = 0$$

We solve each equation:
$$x + 4 = 0 \quad \text{or} \quad x - 3 = 0$$
$$x = -4 \quad \text{or} \quad x = 3$$
Both –4 and 3 should be checked in the original equation.

The solutions are –4 and 3. (*The check is left to the student.*)

Example 2: Solve: $4(3x + 1)(x - 4) = 0$

Solution
Since the factor 4 is constant, the only way for $4(3x + 1)(x - 4)$ to be 0 is for one of the other factors to be 0.
That is, $\quad 3x + 1 = 0 \quad or \quad x - 4 = 0$

$$3x = -1 \quad \text{or} \quad x = 4$$
$$x = 4.$$

Check: For −1/3: For 4:
$$4(3x + 1)(x - 4) = 0 \qquad\qquad 4(3x + 1)(x - 4) = 0$$
$$4(3(-1/3) + 1)(-1/3 - 4) = 0 \qquad 4(3(4) + 1)(4 - 4) = 0$$
$$4(0)(-13/3) = 0 \qquad\qquad 4(13)(0) = 0$$
$$0 = 0 \qquad\qquad 0 = 0$$

The solutions are −1/3 and 4. (*The check is left to the student.*)

Example 3: Solve: $3y(y - 7) = 0$

Solution
$$3 \cdot y(y - 7) = 0$$
$$y = 0 \quad \text{or} \quad y - 7 = 0$$
$$y = 0 \quad \text{or} \quad y = 7$$

The solutions are 0 and 7. (*The check is left to the student.*)

Example 4: Solve: $x^2 + 9x = 0$

Solution
Recall that in order to apply the zero property we need to have **something * something = 0**. If we do not have that then, you need to use what you have already learned to create that situation.

Although there is no constant term, because of the x^2-term, the equation is still a quadratic equation. So the first step is to try factoring:
$$x^2 + 9x = 0$$
$$x(x + 9) = 0$$
$$x = 0 \quad \text{or} \quad x + 9 = 0$$
$$x = 0 \quad \text{or} \quad x = -9$$

The solutions are 0 and −9. (*The check is left to the student.*)

Zero Property Exercise
Solve using the zero property
1) $x^2 + 9x = 0$
2) $(x + 4)(x + 9) = 0$
3) $2x(3x - 2) = 0$
4) $x^2 + 7x + 6 = 0$
5) $x^2 - 9x + 14 = 0$
6) $x^2 - 12x = -36$
7) $9x^2 = 49$
8) $14x^2 + 9x + 2 = 10x + 6$
9) $x^2 - 5x = 18 + 2x$
10) $3x^2 + 8x = 9 + 2x$

The Pythagorean Theorem

The **Pythagorean Theorem** is a concept that is use to solve many situations. We will not go through the proof in this material; we will use the result of the proof.

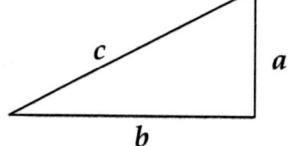

> In any right triangle, if a and b are the lengths of the legs and c is the length of the hypotenuse, then
> $a^2 + b^2 = c^2$.

The **Pythagoras Theorem** simply states that the sum of the squares of the lengths of the sides of a right triangle is equal to the square of the length of the hypotenuse. Thus given any two sides of the triangle we can calculate the third side.

Example: Given that the height of a right triangle is 4 cm and the hypotenuse is 5 cm, find the width of the triangle.

Solution
Since you know the hypotenuse and the height then the formula to use is the Pythagoras theorem
$a^2 + b^2 = c^2$
$4^2 + b^2 = 5^2$
$16 + b^2 = 25$
$b^2 = 25 - 16 = 9$
$b = \pm 3$

Since distance cannot be negative that means that the width of the triangle is 3 cm.

Pythagoras theorem Exercise
Solve the following for a right triangle
1) The height is 6 m and the base is 8 m find the length of the third side.
2) The height is 15 m and the hypotenuse is 21 m find the width.
3) The hypotenuse is 18 m and the base is 7 m find the height.

Zero Property Application
1) *Guy Wire:* The guy wire on a TV antenna is 1m longer than the height of the antenna. If the guy wire is anchored 3m from the foot of the antenna, how tall is the antenna?

2) *Dimension of Picture:* A rectangular picture is twice as long as it is wide. If the area of the picture is 288 in² find its dimensions?

ALGEBRA MADE EASY – A Practical Approach to Algebra

3) **_Measurement:_** A tree house is made with stairs that resembles a 13-ft ladder leaning against the house. The distance from the bottom of the ladder to the base of the tree is 7 ft less than the distance from the top of the ladder to the ground. How far is the bottom of the ladder from the base of the tree?

4) *Gardening:* The Randall's are designing a garden. The garden will be in the shape of a rectangle and have an area of 270 square feet. The width of the garden is 3 feet less than the length. Find the length and width.

5) *Picture Frame:* A frame surrounding a picture is 2 inches wide. The picture inside the frame is 7 inches longer than it is wide. If the overall area of the picture and frame is 198 square inches, find the dimensions of the picture inside the frame.

ALGEBRA MADE EASY UNIT 39
Square Root Property

In this unit we will cover two additional methods for solving quadratic equations. The first of which is the *Square Root Property*.

The *square root property* is a simplified approach used to solve quadratic equations that have no x-terms. That is, no middle term.

To find the *square root* of a number you are looking for a number which when multiplied by itself produces the number in question. Keep in mind that the number that is multiplied can also be negative since a negative number multiplied by another negative number gives a positive result.
    Example $5 \cdot 5 = 25$ and $-5 \cdot -5 = 25$

Let k be any non-negative number. Then the solutions to the equation $x^2 = k$ are given by $x = \pm \sqrt{k}$. If $k < 0$ then the equation will have no real solution since you cannot take the square root of a negative number. Note that the *square root* of a number will have two possibilities; a positive value since a positive times another positive is positive. And a negative value since a negative times another negative give a positive result.

Example: Solve the quadratic equation. $x^2 - 49 = 0$

Solution
We will fist solve this problem using the method that you have been previously taught and then use the square root method.

- Using the Zero Property
    $x^2 - 49 = 0$
    $(x + 7)(x - 7) = 0$
    $x + 7 = 0$ or $x - 7 = 0$
    $x = -7$ or $x = 7$

- Using the square root property
    $x^2 = 49$
    $x = \sqrt{49}$
    $x = \pm 7$

The solutions are –7 and 7; as seen in both cases however the square root method was simpler and quicker.

Square Root Exercise
Solve each equation.
1) $x^2 = 10$
2) $25x^2 - 16 = 0$
3) $(x - 3)^2 = 36$

Completing The Square

The next method to be discussed is called *completing the Square*. *Completing the square* is another method of solving quadratic equations. To complete the square is to create a perfect square trinomial of the form $x^2 + bx + c$. This method is based on the premise that the last term of the perfect square trinomial is the square of one-half of the coefficient of the middle term. Given as

$$x^2 + bx \text{ is } x^2 + bx + (b/2)^2$$

This method is used to solve an equation of the form $Ax^2 + Bx = D$ which cannot be easily factored. After completing the square the expression can be factored easily using the shortcut process.

Example 1: Complete the square for $x^2 - 8x$

Solution
Coefficient of x-term is -8, so we let $b = -8$. To complete the square we divide by 2 and then square the result.

$(b/2)^2 = (8/2)^2 = 4^2 = 16$

The resulting expression becomes $x^2 - 8x + 16$ which can now be factored to be $(x - 4)^2$.

Example 2: Solve $2x^2 - 6x = 4$ by completing the square.

Solution
Step 1: Be sure the squared term has a coefficient of 1. So $2x^2 - 6x = 4$ becomes $2(x^2 - 3x) = 4$
Step 2: Write in correct form. **$(x^2 - 3x + \_\_) = 2 + \_\_$**   *(Divide both sides of the equation by 2)*
Step 3: Complete the square. **$(x^2 - 3x + 9/4) = 2 + 9/4$** $\{(b/2)^2 = (-3/2)^2\}$
Step 4: $(x - 3/2)^2 = 2 + 9/4$
$\qquad (x - 3/2)^2 = 8/4 + 9/4$
$\qquad (x - 3/2)^2 = 17/4$
$\qquad x - 3 = \sqrt{17}/\sqrt{4}$
$\qquad x = \dfrac{3 \pm \sqrt{17}}{2}$

Completing the Square Exercise
Solve by completing the square
1) $x^2 - 8x + 13 = 0$
2) $2x^2 + 8x + 7 = 0$

Concept Application
1) **Driving:** If the braking distance D in feet required to stop a car traveling at x miles per hour on dry, level pavement can be approximated by $D = (1/11)x^2$. If the breaking distance is 50 ft calculate the speed of the car.
Solution at the end of the unit.

Solutions to Concept Application
1) $D = (1/11)x^2$; $50 = (1/11)x^2$. $x^2 = 50*11$; $x = \sqrt{550}$; $x = 23.45$; The car is traveling at 23.45 mph.

ALGEBRA MADE EASY UNIT 40
Quadratic Formula

As you have learned Quadratic equations can be solved by various methods such as factoring, completing the square and even graphing. However, there can be times when neither of those methods will work, therefore an alternate method was devised by a scientist named Newton. This method is known as the Quadratic Formula given as

$$x = \frac{-b \pm \sqrt{b^2 - 4ac}}{2a}$$

Where the symbol "$\pm$" indicates that both

$$\frac{-b + \sqrt{b^2 - 4ac}}{2a} \quad \text{and} \quad \frac{-b - \sqrt{b^2 - 4ac}}{2a}$$

are solutions of the given quadratic equation.

It is important to note that while the other methods can be used at different times to solve quadratic equations; the *quadratic formula* can be used to solve all quadratic equations. However, there are times when another method might be quicker and simpler. You generally use the quadratic formula to find the solution of an equation when you cannot factor the equation; **that is the equation is prime**.

There are also some unique characteristics about the quadratic formula that can give important information about the nature of the solutions. For example, by evaluating the argument **$b^2 - 4ac$** we can tell if the solutions are real, imaginary of if there is only one solution.

The quadratic formula is most commonly used in engineering and science fields where one works a lot with trajectory and estimation. However it is also used in several other areas to design safe and useful products for use.

Let's first look at the formula; later we will look at its characteristics.

To solve a problem using the quadratic equation, fist identify *a*, *b* and *c* and then substitute them into the formula and simplify. *Note that in order to use the quadratic formula the equation that you are solving must be a quadratic equation.*

Determine whether the given equation is quadratic.
  a) $6x + 2x^2 - x^3 = 0$ b) $8 + 7x^2 + 2 = 6x^2 + x$

Solution
a) The equation $6x + 2x^2 - x^3 = 0$ is not quadratic because it has an x^3-term.
b) The equation is quadratic because it can be written in the form $ax^2 + bx + c = 0$ with $a = 1$, $b = -1$, and $c = 10$.

Quadratic Equation Example1: Solve the equation $4x^2 + 3x - 8 = 0$

Solution
Step 1: $a = 4$, $b = 3$ and $c = -8$

Step 2: $x = \dfrac{-3 \pm \sqrt{3^2 - 4*4*-8}}{2*4}$

Step 3: $x = \dfrac{-3 \pm \sqrt{9 + 128}}{8}$

$x = \dfrac{-3 + \sqrt{137}}{8}$ or $x = \dfrac{-3 - \sqrt{137}}{8}$

$x \approx 1.1$ or $x \approx -1.8$

Note the approximation because the square root of 137 is recurring.

Let's look at the graph

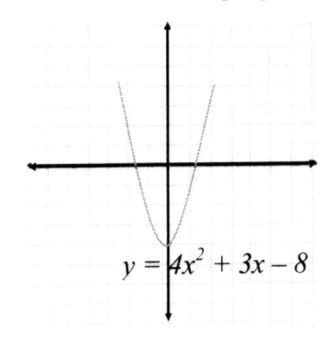

$y = 4x^2 + 3x - 8$

From the graph you can see that the curve crossed the x-axis twice; once at $x = 1.1$ and again at $x = -1.8$. Note that in both of these case $y = 0$ so the points are **(1.1, 0)** and **(-1.8, 0)**.

When you use the quadratic equation to solve for x you are actually finding the x-component of the point where the graph touches, meets or cut the x-axis. Since we equate the equation to zero we are essentially finding the x-intercepts. Note that a point is written in the form *(x, y)*.

Example 2: Solve the equation $25x^2 + 20x + 4 = 0$

Solution
Step 1: $a = 25$, $b = 20$ and $c = 4$

Step 2: $x = \dfrac{-20 \pm \sqrt{20^2 - 4*25*4}}{2*25}$

Step 3: $x = \dfrac{-20 \pm \sqrt{400 - 400}}{50}$

$x = \dfrac{-20}{50}$ Note that $\dfrac{\sqrt{0}}{50} = \dfrac{0}{50}$

$x = -0.4$

There is only one solution which is -0.4.

Let's look at the graph

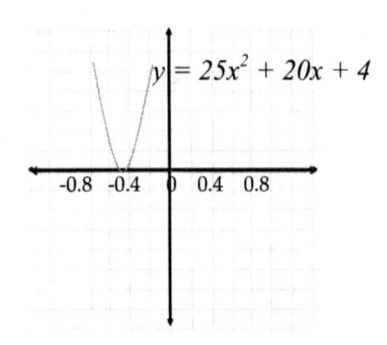

$$y = 25x^2 + 20x + 4$$

From the graph you can see that the curve touched the x-axis only once at $x = -0.4$. The actual point is **(-0.4, 0)**.

Example 3: Solve the equation $5x^2 - x + 3 = 0$

Solution
Step 1: $a = 5$, $b = -1$ and $c = 3$

Step 2: $$x = \frac{-1 \pm \sqrt{-1^2 - 4*5*3}}{2*5}$$

Step 3: $$x = \frac{1 \pm \sqrt{1 - 60}}{10}$$

$$x = \frac{1 \pm \sqrt{-59}}{10}$$

There are no real solutions to this equation because $\sqrt{-59}$ is not a real number. (Later in this unit we will discuss how to find complex solutions to quadratic equations like this one.)

Let's look at the graph

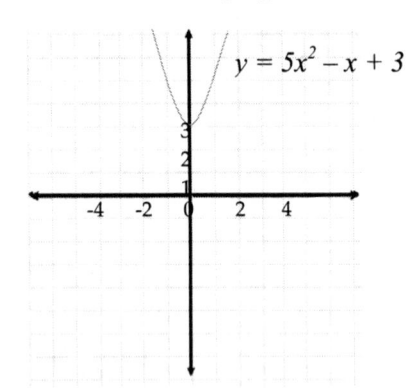

$$y = 5x^2 - x + 3$$

From the graph you can see that the curve never touched the x-axis at any point.

Quadratic Equation Exercise
Solve the equations and support your result graphically.
1) $3x^2 - 6x + 3 = 0$
2) $2x^2 + 4x + 5 = 0$
3) $2x^2 - 3x - 1 = 0$

Characteristics of the Quadratic Equation

We are going to pay attention to the square root portion of the formula since that is the part that has constraints. For example we know that the square root of a negative number is not real so we need to look at the graph based on what is under the square root sign. We call the contents under the square root sign the *discriminant*.

From Examples 1, 2 and 3 we saw the following;
- When the number under the square root was positive, such as with $\sqrt{137}$, there were two points where the graph crossed the x-axis. (*See example 1*). That means that when $b^2 - 4ac$ is > 0 the result is **two solutions**.
- When the number under the square root was equal to zero $\sqrt{0}$ there was only one point where the graph crossed the x-axis. (*See example 2*). That means that when $b^2 - 4ac$ is $= 0$ the result is **one solution**.
- When the number under the square root was negative, such as with $\sqrt{-59}$, there were no points where the graph crossed the x-axis. (*See example 3*). That means that when $b^2 - 4ac$ is < 0 the result is **that there is no real solution**. Or no point of intersection with the x-axis.

Use these concepts you can to determine what the equation could be by looking at the graph.

Example: Match the equation below with its graph.

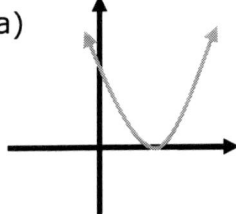

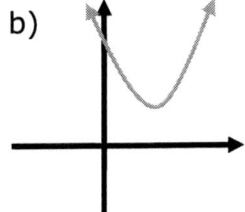

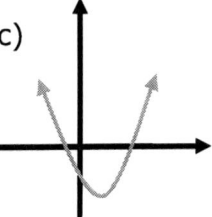

a)   b)   c)

_____ $y = 2x^2 - x + 1$
_____ $y = x^2 - x - 2$
_____ $y = x^2 - 2x + 1$

Solution
Find the result of the *discriminant* in each case and then compare it with the graph.
$$b^2 - 4ac$$
$2x^2 - x + 1;$ $(-1)^2 - 4*2*1 = -7;$ conclusion; there are no real roots so that graph that match is **b**
$x^2 - x - 2;$ $(-1)^2 - 4*1*-2 = 8;$ conclusion; there are real roots so that graph that match is **c**
$x^2 - 2x + 1;$ $(-2)^2 - 4*1*1 = 0;$ conclusion; there is one real roots so that graph that match is **a**

Roots Exercise
Use the discriminant to determine the number of solutions
1) $-2x^2 + 5x = 3$
2) $2x^2 - 5x + 3$
3) $-x^2 + 4x - 7$
4) $x^2 - 6x + 9$

Complex Root

Up until this point you have been told that you cannot take the square root of negative numbers. That is because there are no numbers which multiplied by itself gives a negative number (*Recall that a negative number times another negative number gives a positive result*). That is, every number becomes positive after it is squared.

In order to be able to take the square root of a negative number we are going to have to introduce a new number call *i*; which stand for *"imaginary"*. This new number was invented around the time of the Reformation. At that time, nobody believed that there would be any "*real world*" use for this new number, other than easing the computations involved in solving certain equations. So the new number was viewed as being a pretend number invented for convenience sake.

Today the concept is used mainly in science and research.

The imaginary is defined to be:
$i = \sqrt{-1}$
Then:
$i^2 = (\sqrt{-1})^2 = -1$

Using this number we can now take the square root of negative numbers.

Example $\sqrt{-36} = \sqrt{-1} * \sqrt{36}$

Solution
The square root of 36 is ±6 and since $\sqrt{-1}$ is *i* the result is ±6*i*. The presence of the *i* indicates that you took the square root of a negative number.

Now let's look at finding the solutions of quadratic equation when the roots are negative. The standard format for writing your result is *a + bi*.

Complex Roots Example: Solve $3x^2 - 7x + 5 = 0$. Write your answer in standard form: *a + bi*.

Solution
Step 1: $a = 3, b = -7$ and $c = 5$

Step 2: $x = \dfrac{-(-7) \pm \sqrt{-7^2 - 4*3*5}}{2*3}$

Step 3: $x = \dfrac{7 \pm \sqrt{49 - 60}}{6}$

$x = \dfrac{7 \pm \sqrt{-11}}{6}$

$x = \dfrac{7 + i\sqrt{11}}{6}$ and $x = \dfrac{7 - i\sqrt{11}}{6}$

Complex Root Exercise
Solve the following;
1) $x^2 + 17 = 0$
2) $x(x - 4) = -5$
3) $-2x^2/5 - 3 = -2x$

Key Points
When given an equation to solve
- If it is a linear equation (*that is in the form $Ax + By + C = 0$*) – Use the Additive or the Multiplicative Principle
- If it is a quadratic equation (*that is in the form $Ax^2 + Bx + C = D$*) – Use the zero property, the completing the square method, the square root method or the quadratic formula

---

Concept Application
1) *Sports:* Khal is playing and throws a ball in the air. The ball's height h in feet after t seconds is given by the equations $h = -16t^2 + 48t + 4$. How high will the ball get 3 seconds after Khal throws it?
2) *Gardening:* The length of a rectangular garden is 4ft greater than the width. The area of the garden is 96 ft². Find the length and the width of the garden.

Solutions at the end of this unit.

Solutions to Concept Application
1) $h = -16t^2 + 48t + 4$; $h = -16*3^2 + 48*3 + 4$; $h = 4ft$; the ball will be at a height of 4ft 3 seconds after Khal throws it.
2) Let width = w; $L = w + 4$; Area = 96; Area = $l * w$; $96 = w(w + 4)$; $96 = w^2 + 4w$; $w^2 + 4w - 96 = 0$
    $(w - 12)(w + 8) = 0$; $w = 12$
    The length is 12 in and the width is 8ft.

ALGEBRA MADE EASY UNIT 41
Test 5

Find the GCF
1) x^4y^4, x^3y^2, x^3y^3, xy

Factor the following completely using any method;
2) $4x^2 - 5x + 9$
3) $12x^4 + 17x^2 + 6$
4) $2x^2 - 2x - 12$
5) $x^3 + 6x^2 + 5x + 30$
6) $8a^4b - 18b^3$
7) $x^2 + 4xy - 12y^2$
8) $18m^2 - 17r^3$
9) $x^{10} + 50x^5 + 625$

Solve the following using any process;
10) $7m^2 + 12m + 1 = 0$
11) $6x^2 + 10x = -3$
12) $x^2 - x = 30$
13) $6y^2 + 19y + 10 = 0$
14) $x^2 + 4x - 32 = 0$

15) The height of a box is 5 inches. The length is three inches more than the width. Find the width if the volume is 440 cubic inches.

16) A lot is in the shape of a right triangle. The shorter leg measures 90 meters. The hypotenuse is 30 meters longer than the length of the longer leg. How long is the longer leg?

17) **Distance:** If an object is dropped, the distance it falls is given by $d = 16t^2$. Find the distance an object would fall in 8 seconds.

18) A rectangular garden has dimensions of 19 feet by 14 feet. A gravel path of equal width is to be built around the garden. How wide can the path be if there is enough gravel for 540 square feet?

19) **Picture Frame:** A picture 15 inches by 22 inches is to be mounted on a piece of matboard so that there is an even amount of mat all around the picture. How wide will the border be if the area of the mounted picture is 690 square inches?

20) **Measurement:** A rug is to fit in a room so that a border of even width is left on all four sides. If the room is 15 feet by 21 feet and the area of the rug is 216 square feet, how wide will the border be?

ALGEBRA MADE EASY
Concept Application

Note, when you are asked to demonstrate the use of a concept it does not mean that you mention the concept; it means that you demonstrate how to use that concept by the use of examples showing calculations. Also when ask to select 3 concepts it does not mean that you use one concept and use it 3 times it means that you chose 3 different concepts. These exercises are for you to take and apply what you have learned to create a suitable solution for the project scenario that is presented.

Instructions
1) Select 3 concepts that you have studied that could be applied to the problem stated. Whenever possible translate the information into algebraic equations and solve each equation.
    a. Show ALL details for any calculation of how you arrive at your answer
    b. Show ALL picture(s) and diagrams(s)
- Your response should constitute a complete response to the scenario presented. Where necessary feel free to include additional information pertaining to the specific event to help to generate a complete response.

Activity 1 – Project Management

Imagine that an associate of yours is planning their 50th birthday party and asked you to help with the details. They are planning for about 1000 guests to be in attendance. There is a limit to the time that you will have access to the banquet hall. You will need about 2 hours for set up and the event is expected to last about 5 hours. You will have to be done and out of the banquet hall by 11:59 PM.

They agree to hire help but want to keep the cost to a minimum. You have done events before and have 2 persons that you have used in the past for things like this that you can call on again.

- **One of your help, Nick can take 2 hours to wash 500 dishes, and another help Bren, takes 3 hours to wash 450 dishes. You need to figure out long it will take them working together, to wash all 1000 dishes?**
- **The workers will work at $8.5 per hour for the event. You need an estimate for how much it will cost in salary for the event.**
- **You need to have a solid plan for when to have the workers (hired help) at the banquet hall so that they can get the job done and be out of there on time?**

Plans are to have no more than four workers work the event. All four works will be responsible for serving the meal, washings the dishes and clean up. The meal will be prepared in advance and brought to the banquet hall.

Prepare a detailed schedule for the event. Break down the cost for this event; include any other calculations that you deemed relevant and appropriate. Share this information with the person responsible for paying the bill. The plan should include all the details that will make the event a success.

Activity 2 – Business Opportunity

Imagine that you and a friend are thinking about starting a business in construction. You heard about an opportunity and want to bid for the job. Plans are that the two of you would work on the job and you would hire up to two additional help if needed. You are working on the details for the bid and have some decision to make.

- You have done work like this before and you know that six men could do the job in fourteen days; however the contract is for twenty-one days. Since you have more time you need to figure out how much guys will be needed for the job in order to know if you need to hire anyone and if so how many.
- In this line of work the guys usually work for $21.75 an hour and they usually work 10 hour days; therefore you need to figure out what you will be paying out at in terms of salary.
- In order to ensure that you allow for contingencies, you and your partner decided to include an additional 20% of the cost of the salary in the bid.
- Plans are to charge for materials separately.

You want to ensure that this bid is competitive while at the same time you and your partner want to make money off the job. Estimate the amount of the contract and submit your bid for the job. Your response should detail how you would profit.

Activity 3 – Sales

You are in the energy business as an Independent Energy Consultant and you are working with a potential client Jamie. Jamie is a residential customer that is currently with another company and is approaching the end of her 12 month contract. Jamie needs to decide whether or not to say with her current company or switch to your company. Break it out for Jamie and show her the benefits of going with your company over the competitor.

- Jamie's current plan is as follows and her average monthly usage is about 950 kWh.

Average price per kWh	500 kWh	1000 kWh	2000 kWh
	12.7¢	9.9¢	10.1¢

Contract Term:	12 Months
Monthly Customer Charge to less than 1000 kWh:	$9.99
Energy Charge: (per kWh)	$0.0936
Advanced Metering Charge per month:	$3.05
Delivery Rate Increase per kWh:	$0.00085
Delivery Rate Increase per month:	$1.69
Energy Efficiency per month:	$0.89

- Your Company offers the following plan

Average price per kWh	9.2 for all usage
Contract Term:	12 Months
Cash back rewards (based on 12 months total usage)	2%
Monthly Customer Charge:	$4.95
Energy Charge: (per kWh)	$0.0936

Advanced Metering Charge per month:	$3.05
Delivery Rate Increase per kWh:	$0.00085
Delivery Rate Increase per month:	$1.69
Energy Efficiency per month:	$0.89

Break it down for Jamie and show her the immediate savings that your plan offers then show her the savings after just 6 months and then again after 12 months. Note that in the winter months average energy usage is about 30% lower than in the summer months.

Activity 4 – Business Planning

You work for a finical institution that provides tax and accounting services and guidance for clients. Kalie has a small business and she is your client. She is getting ready to close her books for the end of the year and came to discuss her business finance with you. She bought $3000 computer for that business and estimates the life of the computer at 4 years, after which its value will be $200. While with you Kalie told you about an investment opportunity and asked if you could give her a breakdown of the numbers. Discuss with Kali the options that are available to her to help to make informed decisions.

- **For tax purposes, businesses frequently depreciate equipment. Discuss with Kalie the two methods of depreciation. Do not suggest a method for her; just give her enough information so that she can make her own informed decision.**
- **Discuss with Kalie what you know about compound and simple interest and provide her with a hypothetical example of what a particular investment could potentially be worth after a specified number of years.**

Your job is not to make any decision for Kalie you are just to provide her with some numbers based on your calculations so that she will have information that she can use to make an informed decisions. Be sure to provide her with all the details that support your calculations.

Evaluate yourself and determine how well did you did.

- Did you have difficulties coming up with at least 3 concepts?
- Were you able to relate in any way to any of the problems?

Calculations should be done based on the concepts studied. Complete responses will vary based on numbers selected for some of the scenarios where actual numbers were not given.

ALGEBRA MADE EASY
Appendix

Rules of Operation
These are the rules for working with real numbers

- Positive **plus** Positive = Positive
- Positive **plus** Negative = Take away the smaller from the larger and keep the sign of the larger
- Negative **plus** Negative = Just add the answer will be Negative
- Negative **plus** Positive = Take away the smaller from the larger and keep the sign of the larger
- Negative **minus** Positive = Just add the answer will be Negative
- Negative **minus** Negative = Change sign of the last number to positive and use the rules that applies to positive.
- Positive **minus** Positive = Take away the smaller from the larger and keep the sign of the larger
- Positive **minus** Negative = Just add the answer will be Positive
- Positive **times** Positive = Positive
- Negative **times** Negative = Positive
- Positive **times** Negative = Negative
- Negative **times** Positive = Negative
- Positive **divided by** Positive = Positive
- Negative **divided by** Negative = Positive
- Positive **divided by** Negative = Negative
- Negative **divided by** Positive = Negative

Order of Operation
Not to be confused with the **Rules of Operation** is the **Order of Operation**. When we talk about order relationship we are talking about the order in which the operations must be carried out to produce the desired result.

These few rules will help you to remember how to approach these kinds of questions.
1. Do all the operations inside the **parenthesis** or other grouping symbols **first**.
2. Simplify any expression with exponents and find any square rots
3. Multiply or Divide proceeding form left to right
4. Add or subtract proceeding form left to right
5. Multiplication and Division is always done before Addition and Subtraction.

A simply acronym that you might find easy to remember is PEDMAS
P = Parenthesis
E = Exponents
D = Divisions
M = Multiplication
A = Addition
S = Subtraction

SOLUTIONS AND ANSWERS
To Exercises

Real Number Exercise (Unit 2)
1. 1000065
2. One Hundred, 4 tens and 4 ones or One Hundred and Forty Four.
3. Answer will vary
4. Answer will vary

Number System Exercise (Unit 3)
1. No, negative integers are not natural numbers.
2. Yes, all integers can be written as the quotient of two numbers.
3. Yes, the $\sqrt{9}$ is 3 and 3 is a natural number.
4. $\sqrt{10}$ is an irrational number because it cannot be written as the quotient of two numbers.
5. Yes, are natural numbers are also integers.
6. Yes all whole numbers are real numbers
7. No, not all rational numbers are integers. For example ¾ is a rational number yet it is not an integer.
8. All the numbers are Real Numbers
   Natural Numbers are 5, 16 = 4
   Whole Numbers are 5, $\sqrt{16}$ = 4, 0
   Integers are 5, $\sqrt{16}$ = 4, -27, 0
   Rational Numbers are 5, ½, $\sqrt{16}$=4, 3/7, -27, 0
   Irrational Numbers are $\sqrt{11}$

Whole Numbers Addition Exercise (Unit 4)
1. 565 + 84 = 649
2. 106 + 94 = 200

Whole Numbers Subtraction Exercise (Unit 4)
1. 500 - 84 = 416
2. 250 - 94 = 156

Whole Numbers Multiplication Exercise (Unit 4)
6. 222 x 16 = 3552
7. 19 x 35 = 665
8. 68 x 76 = 5168
9. 56 x 1 = 56
10. 634 x 0 = 0

Whole Numbers Division Exercise (Unit 4)
6. 21 ÷ 4 = 5 remainder 1
7. 35 ÷ 5 = 7
8. 631 ÷15 = 42 remainder 1
9. 5/0 = Undefined
10. 0/35 = 0

Negative Numbers Exercise (Unit 5)
1) -$687.63
2) $23.46
3) -10
4) -150
5) 300

Properties of real Number Exercise (Unit 6)
1. $3 + 4^2 – 5 = 3 + 16 – 5 = 14$
2. $21/7 + 4 – 3*2 = 3 + 7 – 6 = 4$
3. $2(5)^2 – 10) + 4 * 3 ÷ 2 = 2(25 – 10) + 12 ÷ 2 = 2(15) + 6 = 30 + 6 = 36$
4. $21 ÷ 3 + 7 = 7 + 7 = 14$
5. $3 – 2 + 35 ÷ 7 = 3 – 2 + 5 = 6$

Operation Exercise (Unit 6)
1) -5 = 5
2) 0 = 0
3) 75 = 75
4) $-3 – (-5) – 9 + 4 – (-6) = -3 + 5 – 9 + 4 + 6 = 3$
5) $2(-4)^3 - 9(-10) + 3 = 2(-64) + 90 + 3 = -128 + 90 + 3 = -35$
6) $30 ÷ \{5^2/(7-12)\} - (-9) = 30 ÷ \{ 25/(-5)) + 9 = 30 ÷ -5 + 9 = -6 + 9 = 3$
7) $[37 + 15 ÷ (-3)]/2^4 = [37 – 5]/16 = 32/16 = 2$
8) $13x - 5[10x - 7y - (3x - 15y)] = 13x – 5[10x – 7y – 3x + 15y] = 13x – 5[7x + 8y] = 13x – 35x – 40y = -22x – 40y$

Fractions Addition Exercise (Unit 7)
Simplify the following;
7. 4/9 + 2/9 = 6/9 = 2/3
8. 6/15 + 4/15 = 10/15 = 2/3
9. 5/2y + 3/2y = 5/2y
10. 5/6 + 2/3 = 5/6 + 4/6 = 9/6
11. 8 + 7/26 = 8/1 + 7/26 = 208/26 + 7/26 = 215/26
12. 9/a + 5/2a = 18/2a + 5/2a = 23/2a

Fractions Subtraction Exercise (Unit 7)
1. 4/7 - 2/7 = 2/7
2. 6/25 - 4/25 = 2/25
3. 5/3y - 3/3y = 2/3y
4. 5/6 - 1/3 = 5/6 – 2/6 = 4/6 = 2/3
5. 6 - 7/25 = 6/1 – 7/25 = 150/25 – 7/25 = 143/25
6. 9/x - 5/3x = 27/3x – 5/3x = 22/3x

ALGEBRA MADE EASY – A Practical Approach to Algebra

Fractions Multiplication Exercise (Unit 7)
5. 4/5 * 2/7 = 10/35
6. 6/13 * 1/2 = 6/26
7. 5/6 * 1/6 = 5/36
8. $5/x * 3/3x = 15/3x^2$

Fraction Division Exercise (Unit 7)
6. 4/7 ÷ 2/7 = 5/7 * 7/2 = 35/14 = 5/2
7. 6/25 ÷ 4/25 = 6/25 * 25/4 = 150/100 = 3/2
8. $2/5 ÷ 3/5x = 2/5 * 5x/3 = 10x/15 = 2x/3$
9. 5/6 ÷ 1/3 = 5/6 * 3/1 = 15/6 = 5/2
10. 6 ÷ 7/25 = 6/1 * 25/7 = 150/25 = 6

Conversion Exercise (Unit 8)
1) 6*8 = 48; 48 + 3 = 51; keep the denominator gives 51/8
2) 8*3 = 24; 24 + 2 = 26; keep the denominator gives 26/3
3) 9/4 = 2¼
4) 174/8 = 2¾

Add Mixed Numeral Exercise (Unit 8)
1) 4 ⅔ + 3 (4/5); 4+3=7; ⅔ + (4/5) = 10/15 + 12/15 = 22/15 = 7 + 1(7/15) = 8(1/15)
2) 2(5/6) + 5(5/6); 2 + 5 = 7; 5/6 + 5/6 = 10/6= 1⅔; 7 + 1⅔ = 8⅔
3) 3(2/5) + 8(7/10); 3 + 8 = 11; 2/5 + 7/10 = 4/10 + 7/10 = 11/10 = 1(1/10); 11 + 1(1/10) = 12(1/10)

Subtract Mixed Numeral Exercise (Unit 8)
1) 10(5/6) – 4(2/5); 10 – 4 = 6; 5/6 – 2/5 = 25/30 – 12/30 = 13/30; 6 + 13/30 = 6(13/30)
2) 8(1/9) – 3(5/6); 8 – 3 = 5; 1/9 – 5/6 = 2/18 – 15/18 not possible so borrow 1 = 20/18 – 15/18 = 5/18; 5-1 that was borrowed + 5/18 = 4(5/18)
3) -3(1/5) – 4(1/6); 3 – 4=-7; 1/5 – 1/6 = -6/30 – 5/30 = -11/30; -7 + -11/30 = -7(11/30)

Multiply mixed numeral Exercise (Unit 8)
1) 2(1/7) • 3(3/5) = 15/7 • 18/5 = 54/7
2) 3(1/3) • 2½ = 10/3 •5/2 = 8(1/3)
3) 8 • 3½ = 8/1 • 7/2 = 56/2 = 28

Divide mixed numeral Exercise (Unit 8)
1) 2¼ ÷ 1(1/5) = 9/4 ÷ 6/5 = 9/4 •5/6 = 1(7/8)
2) 1¾ ÷ -2½ = 7/4 ÷ -5/2 = 7/4 • -2/5 = -7/10

Application (Unit 8)
1) 11/12 – 1/8 ; 22/24 – 3/24; 19/24; **19/24 of Parmesan cheese remains in the container.**

Decimal Addition Exercise (Unit 9)
1) 4576 + 17.892 = 4593.892
2) –4.207 + (–3.851) = 8.058
3) 1.06 + 9 = 10.06
4) 2.3 + 0.769 + 23 = 26.069

Subtraction Exercise (Unit 9)
1) 36.2 – 16.28 = 19.92
2) 2)1 - 0.0098 = 0.9902

Multiplication Exercise (Unit 9)
1) 7.3 × 85.1 = 6 2 1.2 3
2) 0.0042 × 3215 = 1 3 . 5 0 3 0
3) 5.7 x 0.9 = 5.13
4) 87 x 0.006 = 0.522

Dollars to Cents Conversion Exercise (Unit 9)
1) $189.64 = 18,964¢
2) $0.83 = 83¢

Multiply By Multiplies of 10 Exercise (Unit 9)
1) 100 × 5.1 = 510
2) 1000 × (–2.3046) = –2304.6

Cents to Dollars Conversion Exercise (Unit 9)
1) 343¢ = $3.43
2) 8503¢ = $85.03

Decimal Division Exercise (Unit 9)
1) 91.26 ÷ 26 = 3.51
2) 5.98 ÷ 2 = 2.99
3) 7.872 ÷ (–9.6) = -0.82
4) 5 ÷ 11 = $\overline{0.45}$

Division by Multiples of 10th Exercise (Unit 9)
1) 0.3472 ÷ 10 = 0.03472
2) -16.843 ÷ 0.001 = -16,843
3) 562 ÷ 100 = 5.62

Application (Unit 9)
1) Solution
   Total Minutes = 600
   Additional minutes above 450 = 600 – 450 = 150
   Minutes over 50 = 150 – 50 = 100
   Total bill = 39.99 + 50*0.20 + 100*0.15 = 39.99 + 10 + 15 = 64.99
      His bill for the month is $64.99
2) Solution
   The amount is divided into payments of equal size.

The amount of the payment will depend on the number of payments.
In two years there are 12 · 2 = 24 months

Monthly Amount		Total # payment	divided by	Number of payments
m	=	$2826	÷	24

Solve. Carry out the division. $2826 ÷ 24 = $117.75

Check. To check, we first verify that there are 24 months in 2 years. ; 24 ÷ 12 = 2 years. Then $117.75 * 24 = 2826

State. Bridget's monthly payments would be $117.75.

3) **Solution**
Total pay = $896.75
Rate/ hours = $17
Overtime rate = $25.5
Pay for 40 hrs = 17 x 40 = **680**
896.75 – 680 = **216.75**
216.75 / 25.5 = **8.5**
He worked 8.5 hours in overtime

4) **Solution**
Service Charge = $30
Cost/ hour = $37.50
Bill = $123.75
123.75 – 30 = 93.75
93.75/ 37.5 = 2.5
The job took 2.5 hours

Expression & Equation Exercises (Unit 10)
Translate into algebraic expressions
1. Nine less than some number $x - 9$, **where x is the number**
2. Half of a number $½n$, **where n is the number**
3. The difference of two numbers $x - y$, **where x & y are the numbers**
4. One hundred less than the quotient of two numbers $pq - 100$, **where p & q are the numbers**
5. Some number less than 10 $10 - c$, **where c is the number**
6. Three times a number $3x$, **where x is the number**

Test 1 Answer (Unit 11)
1. (a) 5/3, rational number
   (b) √16 = 4, which is a whole number, integer, natural number & rational number
   (c) -200, rational number and integer
   (d) √12 an irrational number
2. (a) 85, composite = 17*5
   (b) 47, prime
   (c) 1, neither
   (d) 21, composite = 7 * 3
3. (a) 25/0 = undefined
   (b) 31*-1 = -31
   (c) 21* 0 = -21
   (d) 108/18 = 6
4. $\frac{x^3 - 1}{2x} = \frac{(-2)^3 - 1}{2(-2)} = \frac{-8 - 1}{-4} = \frac{-9}{-4} = \frac{9}{4}$
5. *four squared decreased by three* = $4^2 - 3 = 16 - 3 = 13$
6. (a) ½ + 5/6 = 3/6 + 5/6 = 8/6
   (b) 3/8 – 5/6 = 9/24 – 20/24 = -11/24
   (c) 9/12 ÷ 3/8 = 9/12 * 8/3 = 2
   (d) 1/3 * 4/5 = 4/15
7. (a) 4*4*4*4 = 4^5 (b) y*y*y*y = y^4
8. (a) $y = 2x - 2$; $x = 15$ gives $y = 2(15) - 2 = 28$
   (b) $y = 4(2x - 1)$ for $x = 5$ gives $y = 4(2*5 - 1) = 4(10 - 1) = 4*9 = 36$
9. (a) $2^3 = 2*2*2 = 8$
   (b) $9^0 = 1$
   (c) $6^1 = 6*1 = 6$
   (d) $3^4 = 3*3*3*3 = 81$
10. (a) 2 > -5
    (b) -8 < -4
11. (a) $2 + (8 - 20 ÷ 2^2) * 3 = 2 + (8 - 20 ÷ 4) * 3 = 2 + (8 - 5) * 3 = 2 + 3*3 = 2 + 9 = 11$
    (b) 6 ÷ 3 – 18 + 5 * 4 = 2 – 18 + 20 = 4
    (c) 4½ • 6⅔ = 30
    (d) (d) 5½ ÷ 2¾ = 2
    (e) (e) 7.91 ÷ 10 = 0.791
12. (a) 5 + (2 + 3) = (5 + 2) + 3, Associative property
    (b) 6x + 3 + 5x = 6x + 5x + 3, Commutative property
    (c) 2 * (5*3) = 2 * 5*3, Associative property
13. (a) $6x + 5x = 11x$
    (b) $4x^2 + 2 - x^2 = 3x^2 + 2$
    (c) $3(2x - 1) + 5x + 10 = 6x - 3 + 5x + 10 = 11x - 7$
14. $1258 + $2485 + $350 - $115 - $42.85 - $475 - $183 = $3277.15
15. Since the wood is 6 inches wide then there is no need to worry about the width. Focus on the amount needed for the 6 inches long. 66 * 6 = 396 inches. Since 12 inches make 1 foot 396/12 = 33 feet of wood is needed.
16. 2¼ + 3⅔ = 5(7/12);
    She purchased 5(7/12) pounds of meat.

Rounding Exercise (Unit 12)
1. 600
2. 90
3. 1000

Rounding and Estimate Exercise (Unit 12)
1. $90/30 = 3$
2. $5 * 60 = 300$
3. $1000/30 = 33.33 \approx 30$

Exponential Exercise (Unit 13)
1. $6^1 = 6$
2. $(-4)^1 = -4$
3. $5^0 = 1$
4. $(-8.2)^0 = 1$
5. $3^4 = 3*3*3*3 = 81$
6. $-4^2 = -1 *4*4 = -16$
7. $2^3 = 2*2*2 = 8$
8. $4^2 = 4*4 = 16$
9. $(-2)^3 = -2*-2*-2 = -8$
10. $5^3 = 5*5*5 = 125$

Product Rule Exercise Solution (Unit 13)
1) $6^2 \cdot 6^7 \cdot 6^3 = 6^{2+7+3} = 6^{12}$
2) $x \cdot x^6 \cdot x^9 = x^{1+6+9} = x^{16}$; writing x as x^1
3) $(w^3z^4)(w^3z^7) = (w^3w^3)(z^4z^7) = w^6z^{11}$

Quotient Rule Exercise Solution (Unit 13)
1) $\dfrac{6y^{14}}{6y^6} = \dfrac{6}{6}y^{14-6} = y^8$
2) $\dfrac{l^7 m^9}{l^3 m} = l^{7-3} m^{9-1} = l^4 m^8$
3) $\dfrac{5^9}{5^3} = 5^{9-3} = 5^6$

Power Rule Exercise Solution (Unit 13)
1) $(a^3)^2 = a^{3*2} = a^6$
2) $(4^2)^2 = 4^{2*2} = 4^4 = 256$
3) $(y^4)^5 = y^{4*5} = y^{20}$

Product to Power Exercise Solution (Unit 13)
a) $(3x)^4 = 3^4 x^4 = 81x^4$
b) $(-2x^3)^2 = (-2)^2(x^3)^2 = 4x^6$
c) $(a^2 b^3)^7 (a^4 b^5) = (a^2)^7 (b^3)^7 a^4 b^5$
$= a^{14} b^{21} a^4 b^5$
$= a^{18} b^{26}$

Quotient to Power Exercise Solution (Unit 13)
1) $\left[\dfrac{w}{4}\right]^3 = \dfrac{w^3}{4^3}$
2) $\left[\dfrac{3}{b^5}\right]^4 = \dfrac{3^4}{b^{5*4}} = \dfrac{81}{b^{20}}$
3) $\left[\dfrac{a}{b}\right]^7 = \dfrac{a^7}{b^7}$

Scientific Notation Exercise (Unit 13)
1. $10593 = 1.0593 \times 10^4$
2. $6798 = 6.798 \times 10^3$
3. $0.5635 = 5.635 \times 10^{-1}$
4. $0.001065 = 1.065 \times 10^{-3}$
5. One billion = 10^9, the chance of winning the mega million is 1/one billion = $1/10^9 = 10^{-9}$

Additive And Multiplicative Property Exercise (Unit 14)
1. $t - 3 = 19$
2. $x + \frac{1}{2} = -3/2$
3. $M + 18 = -13$
4. $6x = 90$
5. $-x = -10$
6. $2/3 = -5/6y$
7. $5x - 4 = 2x + 6$
8. $4x + 7 - 6x = 10 + 3x + 12$, $x = -3$
9. $3x + 5 = 2(7x - 1)$, $x = 7/11$
10. $8.4 - 3.2y = 4.24$, $y = 1.3$

Linear Inequalities Exercise Unit (15)
1) $2x - 7 < -1$
   $2x < 6; x < 3$
2) $5 - 3x < 11$
   $-3x < 6; x > -2$
3) $\frac{1}{2}x - \frac{2}{3} \leq x + \frac{3}{4}$
   LCD = 12
   $6x - 8 < x + 9$
   $5x < 17; x = 17/5$
4) Let the amount for lunch be x
   Total is given by $x + 1.5 + 3.5 < 20$ Note that she does not have to spend the entire $20.
   $x + 5 \leq 20$
   $x \leq 15$
   Serma can spend $15 or less on her lunch.
5) We know that selling price + tax + setup/delivery fee ≤ 500,
   $x + 0.09x + 64 \leq 500$,
   $x + 0.09x \leq 500 - 64$
   $1.09x \leq 436$,
   $x \leq 400$
   This tells us that Kim can afford to buy any dryer less than or equal to $400.
6) *Translate*: Selling price less Commission is Amount of Loan
   $x \quad - \quad 0.06x \quad \geq \quad 142{,}000$
   Solve: $x - 0.06x \geq 142{,}000$
   $1x - 0.06x \geq 142{,}000$
   $0.94x \geq 142{,}000$
   $\overline{0.94} \quad \overline{0.94}$

$x \geq 151{,}063.83$

Check: Find 6% of 151,063.83:
6% of 151,063.83 = (0.06)(151,063.83) = 9063.83
Subtract the commission to find the remaining amount. 151,063.83 – 9063.83 = 142,000.
State: To have enough money to pay off the loan of $142,000 the Dominique must sell the house for at least $151,063.83.

Linear Equations Exercise Unit (16)
1. $x - 25 = 30$, $x = 55$
2. $m + 6 = 10$, $x = 4$
3. $½ = x - ¾$, $x = 7/8$
4. $3x = 15$, $x = 5$
5. $2x - 15 = -4x + 21$, $x = 6$
6. $-4y - 15 = 25$, $y = -10$
7. $1 - 0.6x = 5$, $x = -40/6$
8. $2(x + 3) + 4x = 0$, $2x + 6 + 4x = 0$, $6x = -6$, $x = -1$
9. $2(3y + 2) + 1 = 2(2y - 1)$, $6y + 4 + 1 = 4y - 3$, $2y = -8$, $y = -4$
10. $-(y + 2) + (3y + 2) = -3(y + 1)$, $-y - 2 + 3y + 2 = -3y - 3$, $y = -3/5$

Problem Solving Exercises (Unit 17)
1) $x + 10 = 2x + 3$; $x - x + 10 = 2x - x + 3$; $10 = x + 3$; $10 - 3 = x + 3 - 3$; $7 = x$; $x = 7$
2) Let x represent the number of people enrolled in Medicare in 2000.
   Then, $x + 0.051x = 41.2$; $1.051x = 41.2$; $x \approx 39.2$. Thus, about 39.2 million people were enrolled in Medicare in 2000.

3) Calculate the value of 4% of 950, then add the value to 950. Thus, 4% of 950 = .04(950) = 38. Then, 950 + 38 = $988 per credit.

4) Let x represent the amount of water that should be added. Note that there is no salt in pure water and that we will add the amount of pure water to the 3% salt solution to obtain a 1.2% solution. Therefore, set up the equation so that the amount of salt on both sides of the equation is equal. Thus, $x(0.00) + 20(0.03) = (x + 20)(0.012)$
$$0.00x + 0.6 = 0.012x + 0.24$$
$$0.6 - 0.24 = 0.012x + 0.24 - 0.24$$
$$0.36 = 0.012x$$
$$x = 0.36/.012 = 30$$
Therefore, 30 ounces of water should be added.

5) Let x represent the number of parking hours in the student lot and y represent the number of parking hours in the nearby lot.

Examine the first question and compare the results for x and y.
Therefore, $2.50 + 1x \leq 5$; $2.50 - 2.50 + x \leq 5 - 2.50$; $x \leq 2.50$. Because a partial hour is charged as a full hour, the student could park in the lot for 3 hours.
Then, $1.25y \leq 5$; $1.25y/1.25 \leq 5/1.25$; $y \leq 4$. Therefore, the student could park in this lot for 4 hours. Thus, for $5.00, the student could park for a longer time in the nearby lot.
Now, examine the second question, $2.50 + 1x \leq 11$; $2.50 - 2.50 + x \leq 11 - 2.50$; $x \leq 8.50$. Because a partial hour is charged as a full hour, the student could park in the lot for 9 hours.
Then, $1.25y \leq 11$; $y \leq 11/1.25$; $y \leq 8.8$ Because a partial hour is charged as a full hour, the student could park in this lot for 8 hours. Thus, for $11.00, the student could park for a longer time in the first lot.

6) **Solution**
   (a) $C = 1.5x + 2000$
   (b) $R = 12x$
   (c) $P = 12x - (1.5x + 2000)$; $P = 10.5x - 2000$
   (d) To yield a positive profit, revenue must be greater than cost. Then, $12x > 1.5x + 2000$; $12x - 1.5x > 1.5x - 1.5x + 2000$; $10.5x > 2000$; $x > 2000/10.5$; $x > 190.476$. Thus, 191 or more compact discs must be sold to turn a profit.

Formula Exercises (Unit 18)
4. $F = 9/5 \cdot C + 32$
5. $c = 4a - 8b$
6. $r = \sqrt{A/\pi}$ or $r = \sqrt{A}/\sqrt{\pi}$

Problem Solving Exercises (Unit 18)
1. Discount = Rate of discount × Original price
   D = 25%   ×   875
   D = 0.25   ×   875
   D = 218.75
   Sale price = Original price – Discount
        = 875 – 218.75
        = 656.25
   The discount amount is $218.75 and the sale price of the couch is $656.25

2. Let the original price for the coat be **x**,
   The sale price can then be written as **x – 0.25x**

To Calculate the Sale Price we are going to use the formula **List Price – Discount = Selling Price**

Since we are told that the sale price is $87

List Price – Discount = Selling Price

$$x - 0.25x = 87$$
$$0.75x = 87$$
$$x = 116$$

The original price of the coat was $116 and the discount is $29.

3. $A = P \cdot (1 + r/n)^{nt}$
   $P = 2000, n = 1, t = 52, r = 0.03$
   $A = 2000(1 + 0.03)^{52 \cdot 1} = 2000(1.03)^{52} = 2000 \cdot 4.65088 = 9301.77$
   The account will have $9301.77 in it.

4. She was going to spend $21 for 2 items
   If she spend $21 to buy the lotion and the body was she will get a 3rd item resulting in an average cost of $7 each
   If she buys 3 items that will be a cost of $31.50 but she also get 2 additional items. Her cost is now over $30 so she can use the coupon and get $10 off brining her cost to $21.50.
   She now has 5 items for $21.50 making that an average of $4.30 each. **If she spends an additional 50 cents buy 3 items with the coupon and the promotion she gets a better deal.**

5. Solution
   Store A
   $60 * 20% off = $12
   $60 - $12 = $48
   $60 - $48 = $12 in savings **Final Price $48 for a total savings of $12 off the original price.**
   Store B
   $55 original price
   $50 sale price w/ 10% off = $5
   $50 - $5 = $45
   $55 - $45 = $10 in savings **Final Price $45 for a total savings $10 off the original price.**
   If only price is considered then store B is giving the better deal.

6. (a) After 0 hours he is where he started which is 4 miles
   After 1 hour he is where he started which is 4 + 8 = 12 miles away
   After 2 hours he is where he started which is 4 + 16 = 20 miles away
   After 3 hours he is where he started which is 4 + 24 = 28 miles away
   After 4 hours he is where he started which is 4 + 32 = 36 miles away
   (b) $D = st + D_0$, $D = 8t + 4$
   (c) When t = 3, D = 3*8 + 4 = 24 + 4 = 28, yes it agrees
   (d) When D = 22, 22 = 8t + 4, 18 = 8t, t = 18/8, t = 9/4 hours.

Test 2 Answers (Unit 19)

1) $40 + $40 = $80
2) Results may vary; One possibility is A swing set ≈ $400. A doll ≈ $40.
3) 3 Swing set ≈ $1200; 7 Doll ≈ $280; Total ≈ $1480. **One possibility is to purchase 3 swing set and 7 dolls.**
4) 3.965×10^3
5) 5.6×10^{-3}
6) $x \leq 30$
7) $x = 2$
8) 300 * 31 = 9300; 300 * 19.85 = 5955; 5955 – 9300 = -3345. **She has a loss of $3345.**
9) Let x represent the amount of water that should be added. Note that there is no hydrochloric acid in pure water and that we will add the amount of pure water to the 15% solution to obtain a 2% solution. Therefore,
   set up the equation so that the amount of hydrochloric acid on both sides of the equation is equal. Thus,
   $x(0.00) + 50(0.15) = (x + 50)(0.02)$;
   $0.00x + 7.5 = 0.02x + 1$;
   $7.5 - 1 = 0.02x + 1 - 1$;
   $6.5 = 0.02x$;
   $6.5 / 0.02 = 0.02x / 0.2$
   $325 = x$
   Therefore, 325 ml of water should be added.

10) Let x represent the number of hours parked after the first half hour. We see that there is a $2.00 cost for the first half hour and $1.25 cost for each hour after that. Therefore,
    $2 + 1.25x \leq 8$; $2 - 2 + 1.25x \leq 8 - 2$; $1.25x \leq 6$; $x \leq 6/1.25$; $x \leq 4.8$
    This result would indicate that the student can park for as long as 4.8 hours beyond the first half hour for $8.00. However, because a partial hour of parking is charged as a full hour, the longest amount of time that the student could park for $8.00 is 4.5 hours.

Geometry Exercises Answers (Unit 20)

1) The figure is made up of a triangle and rectangle. Calculate the area of each. $A_{triangle}$ = ½ bh
   $$½ *15*10 = 75 \text{ ft}^2$$
   A_{square} = bh
   $$15*12 =180 \text{ ft}^2$$
   Total area = 180 ft² + 75 ft² = 255 ft²

2) *Familiarize:* Make a drawing and let P = the perimeter.
   Translate: The perimeter of the garden is given by $P = 2 \cdot (l + w)$.
   $P = 2 \cdot (120 \text{ ft} + 75 \text{ ft})$.
   Solve: We calculate the perimeter as follows:
   $P = 2 \cdot (120 \text{ ft} + 75 \text{ ft}) = 2 \cdot (195 \text{ ft}) = 390 \text{ ft}$
   Then we multiply by $3.95 to find the cost of the fencing:
   Cost = $3.95 × Perimeter = $3.95 × 390 = $1540.50
   State: **The 390 feet of fencing will cost $1540.50.**

3) Number doors = 3, Number windows = 13
   Dimension of window = 3 x 4
   Perimeter of a window = 2(l + w) = 2(3 + 4)
   = 2(7) = 14 / window
   Total perimeter of window = 14 x 13 = 182 ft.
   Dimension of door = 3 x 7
   Note: We do not need to caulk the bottom of the door
   Perimeter needed for a door = 2l + w
   =2(7) + 3
   = 14 + 3 = 17
   Total perimeter of door = 17 x 3 = 51 ft.
   Total distance to chalk = 51 + 182 = 233
   Each chalk covers 56 ft
   Therefore we need 221/56 = 4.16 tubes of caulks
   Each caulk cost $5.95 therefore we it will cost 5 x $5.95 = **$29.75**

4) Let P = the perimeter.
   Since there is 1/2 a circle replacing the fourth side of a square, we add half the circumference to the lengths of the three line segments.
   $P = 8.2 + 5.6 + 8.2 + ½ *2 *\pi*5.2$
   $\approx 22 + 3.14 * 5.2$
   $\approx 22 + 16.328 \approx$ **38.328 cm**

5) *Familiarize:* Make a drawing, notice that the corners of the box will be visible when the pizza is in place. We let A = the area of the box visible.
   Translate:
   Area of Box minus Area of pizza is Visible Area
   $s \cdot s \quad - \quad \pi \cdot r \cdot r \quad = \quad A$
   Solve: The radius is ½ the diameter, or 7 in.
   $s \cdot s \quad - \quad \pi \cdot r \cdot r \quad = \quad A$
   16 in. · 16 in. – 3.14 · 7 in. · 7 in. ≈ A
   256 in² – 153.86 in² ≈ A
   102.14 in² ≈ A
   State: **When the pizza is in place, about 102.14 in² of the box will be visible.**

6) $V = 4/3*\pi*r^3$
   $\approx 4/3 * 3.14 * 4^3$
   $\approx 267.95 \text{ in}^3$

Rate, Ratio & Proportion Exercise (Unit 21)

Solve the following;
(1) 2/3
(2) 1.2/1.5 = 12/15 = 4/5
(3) The rate of pay is the ratio of money earned per length of time worked which gives 4749.60/12 = 395.8. The student earned $395.80 each week.
(4) 468/18 = 26. The rate is 26 mpg.
(5) 3/x = 9/15, x = 5
(6) y/3 = 20/4, y = 15
(7) 5/8 = x/36, x = 22.5. You need 22.5 ounces of concentrated mix
(8) 1/24.5 = 3.75/m, m = 91.875. The cities are 91.875 miles apart.
(9) 195/13 = 255/T, T = 17. They need 17 teachers.
(10) 40/5000 = 2/250 lbs per square feet

Percent Exercise answers (Unit 22)

1. x = 0.21 * 45, x = 9.45
2. First find the amount; x = 0.20 * 585, x = 117
   Next subtract to get the cost of the computer $585 - $117 = $468, **The computer cost $468**
3. 65 = p* 115, p = 65/115 = 0.56521.
   The percent is 56.52%
4. 35 = 0.60 * x; x = 35/0.60 = 58.33
5. Discount = 40 – 25 = 15
   Percent = 15/40 = 0.375 = 37.5%. **He received 37.5% discount.**
6. The tax is (59.99 + 199.99) * 0.0825 = 21.45
   The tax is $21.45
   b) The Total sales = 21.45 + 259.98 = 281.43
   The total purchase is $281.43
7. Total price = Purchase price + sales tax
   Let purchase price be x
   65.8 = x + 0.0825x
   65.8 = 1.0825x
   x = 60.78   **The total purchase was $60.78**

8. Rephrase: Sales tax is what percent of purchase price?
   Translate: $140 = p \times \$1750$
   Solve: $p = 140/1750$; $p = 0.08$.
   The sales tax rate is 8%
9. Commission = Commission rate × Sales
   $17,340 = r \times 289,000$
   To solve, we divide both sides by 289,000:
   $$\frac{17,340}{289,000} = \frac{r \times 289,000}{289,000}$$
   $0.06 = r$ **His commission rate is 6%**
10. Rephrase: 1890 is 6% of what
    Translate: $1890 = 0.06 * x$, $x = 31500$. **His sales for that week were $31500.**

Interest Exercises Answers (Unit 23)
1. We use the formula $I = P \cdot r \cdot t$:
   $I = P \cdot r \cdot t = \$3500 \times 0.08 \times 1$
   $= \$3500 \times 0.08$
   $= \$280$
   The simple interest for 1 year is $280.
2. We use the formula $I = P \cdot r \cdot t$:
   $I = P \cdot r \cdot t = \$3500 \times 8\% \times 1/4$
   $= 3500 * 0.08 * 0.25$
   The simple interest on $3500 for ¼ year is $70.
   We use the formula $I = P \cdot r \cdot t$:
   $I = P \cdot r \cdot t = \$1500 \times 7\% \times 1/3$
   $= 1500 * 0.07 * 1/3$
   The simple interest on $1500 for 4 months is $35.
3. a) After 1 year, the account will contain 105% of $3000:
   $1.05 \times \$3000 = \$3150$
   b) At the end of the second year, the account will contain 105% of $3150:
   $1.05 \times \$3150 = \$3307.5$
   The amount in the account after 2 years is $3307.50.
4. The interest is compounding is quarterly, so
   $n = 4$.
   $P = \$5000$
   $r = 0.08$
   $t = 3 ½$
   $A = 5000(1 + 0.08/4)^{3½ \cdot 4}$
   $A = 5000 * 1.0175 = 5087.39$
   The amount in the account at the end of the 3 ½ year is $5087.39
5. (a) Multiply the balance of $3216.28 by 2%:
   $0.02 * 3216.28 = \$64.33$,
   Kyla's minimum payment is $64.33
   (b) The amount of interest on $3216.28 at 19.7% for one month is given by
   $I = P*r*t = 3216.28 * 0.197 * 1/12 = 52.80$,

Now to find the amount that was applied to the principle you need to subtract the interest for the month form the amount that was paid.
$\$64.33 - 52.80 = 11.20$,
The amount applied to the principal is $11.20
(c) To find the new balance subtract the amount that was applied to the principal from the balance. $\$3215.28 - 11.20 = 3205.08$. **The new balance is $3205.08**

6. (a) $I = p*r*t = \$165000*0.045*1/12 = \$618.75$
   The portion of their first payment applied to the principal is: $\$800 - \$618.75 = \mathbf{\$81.25}$.
   They would have paid $81.25 towards that principal.
   (b) Over the 30-year period, the total paid will be $60 \times \$700 = \$252,000$.
   The total amount of interest paid over the lifetime of the loan is total paid – loan = $\$252,000 - \$165,000 = \$87,000$. **The total interest paid will be $87,000.**

Intercepts Exercise Answers (Unit 24)
1. $y = 4x - 6$
   Let $x = 0$, $y = -6$, y-intercept $(0, -6)$
   Let $y = 0$, $x = 3/2$, x- intercept $(3/2, 0)$
2. $y = 6x$
   Let $x = 0$, $y = 0$, y- intercept $(0, 0)$
   Let $y = 0$, $x = 0$, x- intercept $(0, 0)$
3. $y = ¼x + 3$
   Let $x = 0$, $y = 3$, y- intercept $(0, 3)$
   Let $y = 0$, $x = 0$, x- intercept $(-12, 0)$

Graph Exercise Answers (Unit 24)
1. $4x - 3y = 12$ 2. $2x + 3y = 6$

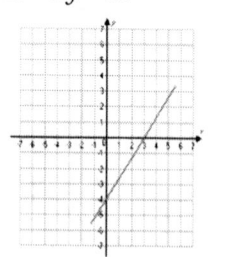

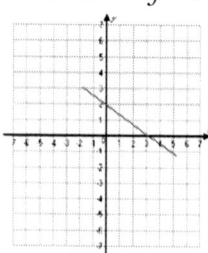

3. $x - 2y = 4$ 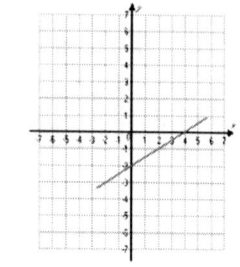   4. $2x + y = 0$

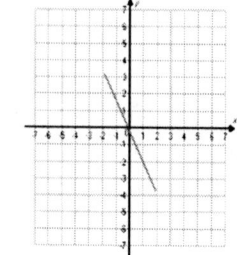

5. $x = -1$ 6. $x = 4$

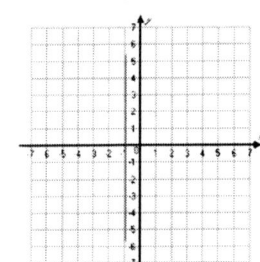

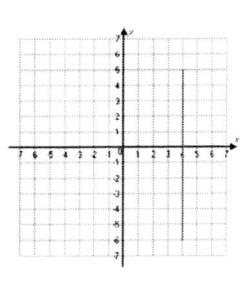

7. $y = 3$ 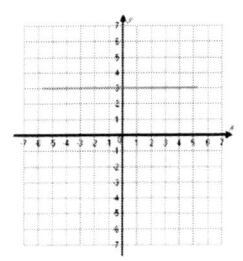   8. $y = -5$

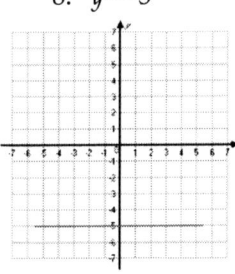

Test 3 Answers (Unit 25)
1) ½ * 4 * 10 = 50   (b) 6*6 = 36 ft²   (c) 3.14 * 6² = 113.04 ft²
2) 6 ¾ ÷ 5 = 1.35 ft.
3) (a) $L = 300x$ (b) $870 = 300x$ (c) $x = 2.9$
4) (a) $h(-3) = (-3)^2 - (-3) = 9 + 3 = 12$
   (b) $h(½) = (½)^2 - (½) = ¼ - ½ = -¼$
   (c) $h(5k) = (5k)^2 - (5k) = 25k^2 - 5k$
5) $b = 2A - h$
6) $0.075x = 1750$; $x = 23333.33$; The car cost approximately $23,333.33.
7) $x + 0.06x = 58300$; $1.06x = 58300$; $x = 55000$; **Her salary before the raise was $55,000.**
8) $h = 20*1 - 5*1^2 = 15$ (b) $h = 20*4 - 5*4^2 = 0$
9) $x = 125 + 125*.08$; $x = 135$; **Next school year tuition be $135 per credit.**
10) Let x represent the interest rate for the $3000 loan and let $x - 0.03$ represent the interest rate for the $5000 loan. The total interest cost for the year will equal the sum of the interest for each loan. Therefore: $3000x + 5000(x - 0.03) = 550$; $3000x + 5000x - 150 = 550$; $8000x - 150 + 150 = 550 + 150$; $8000x = 700$; $x = 700/8000$; $x = 0.0875$
Therefore, the interest rate for the $3000 loan is 8.75% and the interest rate for the $5000 loan is $0.0875 - 0.03 = 0.0575$ or 5.75%.

Introduction to Polynomial Exercise (Unit 26)
1) The coefficient of $5x^4$ is 5.
   The coefficient of $-8x^2$ is –8.
   The coefficient of $2x$ is 2.
   The coefficient of –9 is simply –9.
   The degree of the polynomial is 4

2) The coefficient of $2x^2$ is 2.
   The coefficient of $-4x^3$ is –4.
   The coefficient of 3 is 3.
   The degree of the polynomial is 3
3) The coefficient of $-3x^3$ is 3.
   The coefficient of x^2 is 1, since $x^2 = 1 x^2$.
   The degree of the polynomial is 3

Adding Polynomial Exercise (Unit 27)
(1) $2x + 5y$ (2) $3x^2 + 4x - 2$
   $+ 3x - 2y$ $+ -7x^2 - 10x + 17$
   $5x + 3y$ $-4x^2 - 6x + 15$

(3) $-6x^3 \quad\quad + 7x - 2$ (4) $3 - 4x + 2x^2$
    $+ 5x^3 + 4x^2 \quad + 3$ $-6 + 8x - 4x^2 + 2x^3$
    $-x^3 + 4x^2 + 7x + 1$ $-3 + 4x - 2x^2 + 2x^3$

(5) $10x^5 \quad - 3x^3 + 7x^2 + 4$
              $6x^4 \quad\quad - 8x^2 + 7$
     $+ 4x^6 - 6x^5 \quad\quad + 2x^2 + 6$
     $4x^6 + 4x^5 + 6x^4 - 3x^3 + \; x^2 + 17$

Subtracting Polynomial Exercise (Unit 27)
(1) $x^3 - x^2 + 2x - 12$ (2) $9x^2 + 7x - 2$
     $+ 2x^3 + x^2 + 3x$ $- 2x^2 + 4x + 6$
     $3x^3 \quad\quad + 5x - 12$ $7x^2 + 11x + 4$

(3) $8y^3 - 10y^2 - 14y - 2$ (4) $10x^5 \quad\quad + 2x^3 - 3x^2 + 5$
    $- 5y^3 \quad\quad + 3y - 6$ $+ 3x^5 - 2x^4 + 5x^3 + 4x^2$
    $3y^3 - 10y^2 - 11y - 8$ $13x^5 - 2x^4 + 7x^3 + x^2 + 5$

(5) $8x^5 + 2x^3 - 10x$
    $-4x^5 + 5x^3 \quad\quad - 6$
    $4x^5 + 7x^3 - 10x - 6$

Application (Unit 27)
1) w = 145, h = 68, A = 48
   655 + 4.3*145w + 4.7*68h – 47*48
   655 + 623.5 + 319.6 – 225.6
   = 1372.5   **Answer her daily caloric needs is 1372.5**
2) W= 200, h=74, A = 35
   66 + 6.3w + 12.9h – 6.8A
   66 + 6.3*200 + 12.9*74 – 6.8*35
   66 + 1260 + 954.60 – 238
   = 2040.60   **Answer his daily caloric needs is 2040.60**
3) A = 28, h = 175 cm
   C = 0.041(175) – 0.018(28) – 2.69 =
   7.175 – 0.504   – 2.69 = 3.981
   The person's lung capacity is 3.981 liters

4) $A = 28$, $h = 175$ cm
$C = 0.041(175) - 0.018(28) - 2.69 =$
   $7.175 - 0.504 - 2.69 = 3.981$
The person's lung capacity is 3.981 liters

Multiplying Monomial Exercise (unit 28)
1) $(6x)(7x) = (6 \cdot 7)(x \cdot x) = 42x^2$
2) $(5a)(-a) = (5a)(-1a) = (5)(-1)(a \cdot a) = -5a^2$
3) $(-8x^6)(3x^4) = (-8 \cdot 3)(x^6 \cdot x^4) = -24x^{6+4} = -24x^{10}$
4) $x(x + 7) = x \cdot x = x^2 + 7x$
5) $6x(x^2 - 4x + 5) = 6x^3 - 24x^2 + 30x$

Multiply Monomial and Polynomial Exercise (Unit 28)
1) $(x + 3)(x + 5) = x(x + 5) + 3(x + 5)$
   $= x \cdot x + x \cdot 5 + 3 \cdot x + 3 \cdot 5$
   $= x^2 + 5x + 3x + 15$
   $= x^2 + 8x + 15$

2) $(3x - 2)(x - 1) = 3x(x - 1) - 2(x - 1)$
   $= 3x \cdot x - 3x \cdot 1 - 2 \cdot x - 2(-1)$
   $= 3x^2 - 3x - 2x + 2$
   $= 3x^2 - 5x + 2$

3) $(x + 8)(x + 5) = x(x + 5) + 8(x + 5)$
   $= x \cdot x + x \cdot 5 + 8 \cdot x + 8 \cdot 5$
   $= x^2 + 5x + 8x + 40$
   $= x^2 + 13x + 40$

4) $(x + 5)(x - 4) = x(x - 4) + 5(x - 4)$
   $= x \cdot x + x \cdot -4 + 5 \cdot x + 5 \cdot -4$
   $= x^2 - 4x + 5x - 20$
   $= x^2 + x - 20$

Product of Two Polynomials Exercise (Unit 28)

1) $3x + 7$
    $\underline{\quad x - 2\quad}$
    $-6x - 14$
    $\underline{3x^2 + 7x\quad}$
    $3x^2 + x - 14$

(2) $p^2 + 3p - 2$
     $\underline{\quad p + 2}$
     $2p^2 + 6p - 4$
     $\underline{p^3 + 3p^2 - 2p\quad}$
     $p^3 + 5p^2 + 4p - 4$

(3) $x^3 - 4x^2 + 3x - 5$
     $\underline{\quad\quad 5x^2 + \quad 2}$
     $2x^3 - 8x^2 + 6x - 10$
     $\underline{5x^5 - 20x^4 + 15x^3 - 25x^2\quad}$
     $5x^5 - 20x^4 + 17x^3 - 33x^2 + 6x - 10$

4) $2z^3 - 3z^2 + 4$
    $\underline{\quad -2z - 3}$
    $-6z^3 + 9z^2 \quad -12$
    $\underline{-4z^4 + 6z^3 \quad -8z\quad}$
    $-4z^4 + 9z^2 - 8z - 12$

(5) $-3x^2 + 5x - 2$
     $\underline{\quad -5x - 6}$
     $18x^2 - 30x + 12$
     $\underline{15x^3 - 25x^2 + 10x\quad}$
     $15x^3 - 7x^2 - 20x + 12$

FOIL Method Exercise (Unit 28)
1) $(x + 8)(x + 5) = x^2 + 5x + 8x + 40$
   $\quad\quad\quad\quad\quad\quad\quad = x^2 + 13x + 40$
2) $(y + 4)(y - 3) \quad = y^2 - 3y + 4y - 12$
   $\quad\quad\quad\quad\quad\quad\quad = y^2 + y - 12$
3) $(5t^3 + 4t)(2t^2 - 1) = 10t^5 - 5t^3 + 8t^3 - 4t$
   $\quad\quad\quad\quad\quad\quad\quad\quad = 10t^5 + 3t^3 - 4t$
4) $(4 - 3x)(8 - 5x^3) = 32 - 20x^3 - 24x + 15x^4$
   $\quad\quad\quad\quad\quad\quad\quad = 32 - 24x - 20x^3 + 15x^4$
   $\quad\quad\quad\quad\quad\quad\quad = 15x^4 - 20x^3 - 24x + 32$

Polynomial General Exercise (Unit 28)
1) $(x + 8)(x + 5) = x^2 + 5x + 8x + 40$
   $\quad\quad\quad\quad\quad\quad\quad = x^2 + 13x + 40$
2) $(y + 4)(y - 3) \quad = y^2 - 3y + 4y - 12$
   $\quad\quad\quad\quad\quad\quad\quad = y^2 + y - 12$
3) $(5t^3 + 4t)(2t^2 - 1) = 10t^5 - 5t^3 + 8t^3 - 4t$
   $\quad\quad\quad\quad\quad\quad\quad\quad = 10t^5 + 3t^3 - 4t$
4) $(4 - 3x)(8 - 5x^3) = 32 - 20x^3 - 24x + 15x^4$
   $\quad\quad\quad\quad\quad\quad\quad = 32 - 24x - 20x^3 + 15x^4$
   $\quad\quad\quad\quad\quad\quad\quad = 15x^4 - 20x^3 - 24x + 32$

5) $(3x^5 + 2x^2 + 3x)(2x^2 + 4x)$
   $\quad\quad 3x^5 \quad\quad\quad\quad + 2x^2 + 3x$
   $\underline{\quad\quad\quad\quad\quad\quad\quad\quad 2x^2 + 4x}$
   $\quad 12x^6 \quad\quad\quad + 8x^3 + 12x^2$
   $\underline{\quad 6x^7 \quad\quad + 4x^4 + 6x^3\quad\quad}$
   $6x^7 + 12x^6 + 4x^4 + 14x^3 + 12x^2$

6) $(x + 9)(x + 9) = x^2 + 18x + 81$
7) $3x^2(4x^2 + x - 2) = 12x^4 + 3x^3 - 6x^2$
8) *Manufacturing*
   $V = l*w*h$
   $V = (x + 8)*(x)*(x + 1)$
   $= (x^2 + 8x)(x + 1)$
   $= x^3 + x^2 + 8x^2 + 8x$
   $= x^3 + 9x^2 + 8x$

9) *Lawn Space*
   Rewording: Area of — Area of — Area
   $\quad\quad\quad\quad\quad$ lawn — shed = left over
   Translating: x ft · x ft − 8 ft · 8 ft = Area left over
   Solve: $\quad x^2$ ft^2 − 64 ft^2 = Area left over.
   Check: As a partial check, note that the units in the answer are square feet, a measure of area, as expected.
   State: **The remaining area in the yard is $(x^2 - 64)$ ft^2.**

Binomial Square Exercise (Unit 29)
$(A + B)^2 = A^2 + 2 \cdot A \cdot B + B^2$
1) $(x + 8)^2 = x^2 + 2 \cdot x \cdot 8 + 8^2$
   $\quad\quad\quad\quad = x^2 + 16x + 64$

ALGEBRA MADE EASY – A Practical Approach to Algebra

2) $(3x + 5)^2 = (3x)^2 + 2 \cdot 3x \cdot 5 + 5^2$
   $= 9x^2 + 30x + 25$

3) $(y - 7)^2 = y^2 - 2 \cdot y \cdot 7 + 7^2$
   $= y^2 - 14y + 49$

4) $(4x - 3x^5)^2 = (4x)^2 - 2 \cdot 4x \cdot 3x^5 + (3x^5)^2$
   $= 16x^2 - 24x^6 + 9x^{10}$
   $= 9x^{10} - 24x^6 + 16x^2$

Difference of Squares Exercise (Unit 29)

$(A + B)(A - B) = A^2 - B^2$

1) $(x + 8)(x - 8) = x^2 - 8^2 = x^2 - 64$
2) $(6 + 5w)(6 - 5w) = 6^2 - (5w)^2 = 36 - 25w^2$
3) $(4t^3 - 3)(4t^3 + 3) = (4t^3)^2 - 3^2 = 16t^6 - 9$

Multiply Polynomial Exercise (Unit 29)

1) (a) $(x + 5)(x - 5) = x^2 - 25$
2) b) $(w - 7)(w + 4) = w^2 + 4w - 7w - 28 = w^2 - 3w - 28$
3) $(x + 9)(x + 9) = x^2 + 18x + 81$
4) $3x^2(4x^2 + x - 2) = 12x^4 + 3x^3 - 6x^2$
5)
   $p^2 + 3p - 2$
   $\underline{\quad\quad p + 2}$
   $2p^2 + 6p - 4$
   $\underline{p^3 + 3p^2 - 2p\quad}$
   $p^3 + 5p^2 + 4p - 4$

6) $(2x + 1)^2 = 4x^2 + 2(2x)(1) + 1 = 4x^2 + 4x + 1$

Divide Monomial Exercise (Unit 30)

1) $x^3 - 6x^2 + 9x + 3 \div -3 = x^3/3 - 6x^2/3 + 9x/3 + 3/3$
   $= x^3/3 - 2x^2 + 3x + 1$

2) $2x^6 - 8x^3 + 12x^2 + 24x \div 2x = 2x^6/2x - 8x^3/2x + 12x^2/2x + 24x/2x = x^{6-1} - 4x^{3-1} + 6x^{2-1} + 12x^{1-1}$
   $= x^5 - 4x^2 + 6x + 12$

3) $\dfrac{x^5 + 24x^4 - 12x^3}{6x} = \dfrac{1}{6} x^{5-1} + \dfrac{24}{6} x^{4-1} - \dfrac{12}{6} x^{3-1}$
   $= 1/6 \, x^4 + 4x^3 - 2x^2$

4) $-8x^6 + 12x^4 - 4x^2 \div 4x^2 = -8x^6/4x^2 + 12x^4/4x^2 - 4x^2/4x^2$
   $= -2x^{6-2} + 3x^{4-2} - 1x^{2-2} = -24^2 + 3x^2 - 1$

5) $25x^9 - 7x^4 + 10x^3 \div 5x^3 = 25x^9/5x^3 - 7x^4/5x^3 + 10x^3/5x^3$
   $= 5x^{9-3} - 7/5x^{4-3} + 2x^{3-3} = 5x^6 - 7/5x^3 + 2$

6) $18x^7y^6 - 6x^2y^3 + 60xy^2 \div 6xy^2 = 18x^7y^6/6xy^2 - 6x^2y^3/6xy^2 + 60xy^2/6xy^2 = 3x^{7-1}y^{6-2} - x^{2-1}y^{3-2} + 10x^{1-1}y^{2-2}$
   $= 3x^6y^4 - xy + 10$

7) $-9ab^2 - 6a^3b^3 \div -3ab^2 = -9ab^2/-3ab^2 - 6a^3b^3/-3ab^2$
   $= -9/-3 \, a^{1-1}b^{2-2} - 6/-3a^{3-2}b^{3-2} = 3 + 2ab$

8) $21a^5b^4 - 14a^3b^2 + 7a^2b \div -7a^2b = \dfrac{21a^5b^4 - 14a^3b^2 + 7a^2b}{-7a^2b}$
   $= \dfrac{21a^5b^4}{-7a^2b} - \dfrac{14a^3b^2}{-7a^2b} + \dfrac{7a^2b}{-7a^2b}$
   $= \dfrac{-21}{7} a^{5-2}b^{4-1} + \dfrac{14}{7} a^{3-2}b^{2-1} + \dfrac{7}{7}$

$= -3a^3b^3 + 2ab - 1$

Divide by Polynomial Exercise (Unit 30)

1) $(x^2 - 3x + 1) \div (x - 2) = 2x + 1 + 3/(x - 2)$
2) $(x^3 - x + 2) \div (x - 2) = 4x + 1 + 21/(x + 2)$
3) $(2x^3 + 3x^2 + 3x - 1) \div (2x + 1) = x^2 + x + 1 - 2/(2x + 1)$
4) $(x^4 - x^3 + x^2 - x + 1) \div (x^2 - 1) = x^2 - x + 2 + (-2x + 3)/(x^2 - 1)$
5) $(-3x^3 + 8x^2 + x) \div (3x + 4) = -x^2 + 4x - 5 + 20/(3x + 4)$

Application of Polynomials (Unit 30)

1) $V = Ah$
   $2x^3 + 4x^2 = 2x^2h$
   $h = \dfrac{2x^3 + 4x^2}{2x^2} = x + 2$

2) (a) $t^2 + 60 = 0^2 + 60 = 60$ bmp
   (b) $t^2 + 60 = 10^2 + 60 = 100 + 60 = 160$ bmp
   (c) It increases

3) $P(1 + 0.06)^3 = P(1.06)^3 = P(1.191016)$; let $P = \$700$
   that gives $700(1.191016) = \$833.71$

4) (a) $20t$
   (b) $2t + 2000$
   (c) $(20t) - (2t - 2000) = 20t - 2t - 2000 = 18t - 2000$; profit from selling t tickets.

5) (a) $t(96 - 16t) = 96t - 16t^2$
   (b) $t = 2$ gives $96(2) - 16(2)^2 = 192 - 64 = 128$; that means that after 2 seconds the ball is 128 feet thigh.

6) (a) $t(88 - 16t) = 88t - 16t^2$
   (b) $t = 3$ gives $88(2) - 16(3)^2 = 264 - 144 = 120$; that means that after 3 seconds the ball is 120 feet thigh.

7) (a) 239 million = 2.39×10^8
   (b) $(2.31)(2.39 \times 10^8) = (2.31)(2.39) \times 10^8 = 5.5209 \times 10^8$ gal or 552,090,000 gal

8) (a) 2.19 trillion = 2.19×10^{12}, 249 million = 2.49×10^8

9) Let x represent the amount of 3% cranberry concentrate, then the 5% cran-raspberry concentrate is the sum of the of 3% cranberry concentrate and the 6% raspberry juice concentrate . Therefore
   $0.03x + 0.06 \cdot 400 = 0.05(x + 400)$
   $0.03x + 24 = 0.05x + 20$
   $4 = 0.02x =$
   $x = 200$

The result is that 200 milliliter of 3% cranberry juice concentrate should be added to 400

milliliters of a 6% raspberry juice concentrate to make a 5% cran-raspberry concentrate.

Test 4 (Unit 31)
1) -17
2) Monomial, degree 1
3) 5,2,0,3 The degree of the polynomial is 5
4) $(3x + 4) + (6x + 2) = 9x + 6$
5) $y^6 \cdot y^0 = y^6$
6) $(8 + 3x^5 + 6x^4) + (6x^5 - 8x^4 - 3) = 9x^5 - 2x^4 + 5$
7) $(9x^8 - 8x^5 + 5x^2 + 9) + (9x^7 + 2x^5 - 5x) = 9x^8 + 9x^7 - 6x^5 + 5x^2 - 5x + 9$
8) $(4k - 5)(3k^3 - 2k^2 - 3k + 4) = 12k^4 - 23k^3 - 2k^2 + 31k - 20$
9) $10x^7(8x^3 + 5x^2) = 80x^{10} + 50$
10) 1
11) $(3/5 - 6x^4)(3/5 + 6x^4) = 9/25 - 36x^8$
12) $(25x + 18xy - 21y) - (28x - 8xy - 24y) = -3x + 26xy + 3y$
13) $(6 - 7x^3 + 5x^5 + 3x^4) + (6x^4 - 3x^3 + 8 + 8x^5) = 13x^5 + 9x^4 - 10x^3 + 14$
14) $3x^6 - 17x^5 - 6$
15) $(2x + 10)(x + 4) = 2x^2 + 18x + 40$
16) $8x^4 - 5x - 4$
17) $3x^8 - x$
18) 3 liters
19) $9000
20) 224 feet

GCF Exercise (Unit 33)
1) $9a - 21 = 3 \cdot 3a - 3 \cdot 7$ Factoring each term
   $= 3(3a - 7)$ Factoring out the GCF, 3
2) $28x^6 + 32x^3 = 4x^3 \cdot 7x^3 + 4x^3 \cdot 8$ Factoring each term
   $= 4x^3(7x^3 + 8)$ Factoring out the GCF, $4x^3$
3) The GCF is $3x^3$; $12x^5 - 21x^4 + 24x^3$
   $= 3x^3 \cdot 4x^2 - 3x^3 \cdot 7x + 3x^3 \cdot 8 = 3x^3(4x^2 - 7x + 8)$
4) $9a^3b^4 + 18a^2b^3 = 9a^2b^3(ab + 2)$; The GCF is $9a^2b^3$.
5) $-4xy + 8xw - 12x = -4x(y - 2w + 3)$
6) The GCF for $66t$ and $16t^2$ is $2t$ because $66t = 2t * 33$ and $16t^2 = 2t * 8t$
   Therefore this polynomial can be factored as $66t - 16t^2 = \mathbf{2t(33 - 8t)}$.
7) Volume $= 4x^3 - 60x^2 + 200x$
   a) When $x = 3$; $4(3)^3 - 60(3)^2 + 200(3) = 4*27 - 60*9 + 600 = 168$
   b) The GCF is $4x$; $4x(x^2 - 15x + 50)$

Factor by Grouping Exercise (Unit 34)
1) $(xy + 3x) + (-5y - 15) = x(y + 3) - 5(y + 3) = (x - 5)(y + 3)$
2) $x^3(x - 1) + 2(x - 1) = (x^3 + 2)(x - 1)$
3) $(5x^2 + 3)(4x^2 - 5)$
4) $(2x + 4y)(x + 3y)$

Trial & Error Exercise 1 (Unit 35)
1) $(x + 2)(x + 3)$
2) $(x - 2)(x - 4)$
3) $(x + 5)(x - 2)$
4) $(y + 3)(y - 9)$
5) Rewrite the trinomial $t^2 + 4t - 32$. We need one positive and one negative factor. The sum must be 4, so the positive factor must have the larger absolute value. $t^2 + 4t - 32 = (t + 8)(t - 4)$

Positive "c" Exercise (Unit 35)
1) $x^2 - 7x + 10 = (x - 2)(x - 5)$
2) $x^2 - 8x + 15 = (x - 3)(x - 5)$
3) $y^2 - 9y + 18 = (y - 3)(y - 6)$

Negative "c" Exercise Unit 35)
1) $x^2 - 3x - 4 = (x + 1)(x - 4)$
2) $x^2 + 7x - 8 = (x - 1)(x + 8)$
3) $t^2 - 2t - 24 = (t - 6)(t + 4)$

Trial & Error Exercise 2 (Unit 35)
1) $5x^2 - 10x - 40 = 5(x^2 - 2x - 8) = 5(x - 4)(x + 2)$.
2) $2x^2 + 8x - 10 = 2(x^2 + 4x - 5) = 2(x + 5)(x - 1)$.
3) $2t^3 - 6t^2 + 8t = 2t(t^2 - 3x + 4)$

AC-Method Exercise (Unit 36)
1) $8x^3 + 10x^2 - 12x = (x + 2)(4x - 3)$
2) $5x^2 + x - 18 = (5x - 9)(x + 2)$
3) $2x^2 + 7x - 4 = (2x - 1)(x + 4)$
4) $3y^2 + 10y + 3 = (3y + 1)(y + 3)$
5) $5m^2 - 11m + 2 = (5m - 1)(m - 2)$

General Factoring Strategy Exercise (Unit 37)
1. $25t^4 - 625 = 25(t^2 + 5)(t^2 - 5)$
2. $2x^3 + 14x^2 + 3x + 21 = (x + 7)(2x^2 + 3)$
3. $-x^5 - 2x^4 + 24x^3 = -x^3(x - 4)(x + 6)$
4. $x^2 - 18x + 81 = (x - 9)^2$
5. $12x^2y^3 + 20x^3y^4 + 4x^2y^5 = 4x^2y^3(3 + 5xy + y^2)$
6. $ab + ac + wb + wc = (b + c)(a + w)$
7. $36x^2 + 36xy + 9y^2 = (6x + 3y)^2$
8. $a^8 - 16b^4 = (a^2 - 2b^2)(a^2 + 2b^2)$

Zero Property Exercise (Unit 38)
1) $x = 0$ or $x = -9$
2) $x = -4$ or $x = -9$
3) $x = 0$ or $x = 2/3$
4) $x = -6$ or $x = -1$
5) $x = 2$ or $x = 7$

6) $x = 6$
7) $x = 7/3$ or $x = -7/3$
8) $x = 4/7$ or $x = -1/2$
9) $x = -2$ or $x = 9$
10) $x = -3$ or $x = 1$

Pythagoras theorem Exercise (Unit 38)
1) $a^2 + b^2 = c^2$
2) $6^2 + 8^2 = 36 + 64 = 100$, $c = 10$; the hypotenuse is 10m
3) $15^2 + b^2 = 21^2$; $225 + b^2 = 441$, $b^2 = 216$; $b = 14.7$; the base is 14.7m
4) $a^2 + 7^2 = 18^2$; $a^2 + 49 = 324$; $a^2 = 275$; $a = 16.6$; the height is 16.6 m

Zero Property Application (Unit 38)
1) height = a
   B = 3
   hypotenuse = a + 1
   $c^2 = a^2 + b^2$
   $(a+1)^2 = a^2 + 3^2$
   $a^2 + 2a + 1 = a^2 + 9$
   $2a = 9 - 1 \Rightarrow 2a = 8$
   $a = 4$ **Answer The antenna is 4m tall.**
2) Let width = w
   L = 2w
   Area = 288
   Area = $l * w$
   $288 = 2w * w$
   $288 = 2w^2 \Rightarrow w = \sqrt{288}/2$
   $\sqrt{144} = 12$ (note that we only take the positive root because measurement cannot be negative)
   Therefore Length = 24 in and Width = 12 in
3) *Familiarize*: From the drawing you will see that the ladder and the missing dimensions form a right triangle.
   If the distance from top of the ladder to the ground = x
   Then the distance from bottom of the ladder to house = $x - 7$.
   The hypotenuse has length 13 ft.
   Translate: Since a right triangle is formed, we can use the Pythagorean Theorem: $a^2 + b^2 = c^2$
      That gives $x^2 + (x - 7)^2 = 13^2$
   Solve. Finally solve the equation.
   $x^2 + (x - 7)^2 = 13^2$
   $x^2 + (x^2 - 14x + 49) = 169$
   $2x^2 - 14x + 49 = 169$
   $2x^2 - 14x - 120 = 0$
   $2(x^2 - 17x - 60) = 0$
   $2(x - 12)(x + 5) = 0$

$x - 12 = 0$ or $x + 5 = 0$
$x = 12$ or $x = -5$
Check: The integer –5 cannot be a length of a side because it is negative. When $x = 12$, $x - 7 = 5$, and $12^2 + 5^2 = 13^2$. So 12 checks.
State: **The distance from the bottom of the ladder to the house is 5 ft. The distance from the top of the ladder to the ground is 12 ft.**

4) *Step 1* The area of a rectangle is Length · Width.
   Let x = the length, in feet.
   The width is then $x - 3$.
   Step 2 Rewording: The area of the rectangle is 270 ft².
   Translating: $x(x - 3) = 270$
   Step 3 Solve. We solve the equation.
   $x(x - 3) = 270$
   $x^2 - 3x = 270$
   $x^2 - 3x - 270 = 0$
   $(x - 18)(x + 15) = 0$
   $x - 18 = 0$ or $x + 15 = 0$
   $x = 18$ or $x = -15$
   Step 4 Since the length must be positive, –15 cannot be a solution.
   State. **The garden is 18 feet long and 15 feet wide.**

5) Let x be the width of the picture then the length is and $x + 7$.

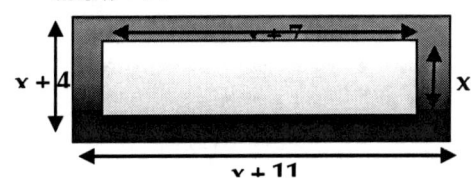

   $(x + 4)(x + 11) = 198$; *the area of picture & frame*
   $x^2 + 15x + 44 = 198$
   $x^2 + 15x - 154 = 0$
   $(x - 7)(x + 22) = 0$
   $x - 7 = 0$ or $x + 22 = 0$
   $x = 7$ or $x = -22$

   The only valid solution for x is 7 inches. Because the length is 7 inches more than the width, the dimensions of the picture are 7 inches and 14 inches.

Square Root Exercise (Unit 39)
1) $x^2 = 10$, $x = \pm\sqrt{10}$
2) $25x^2 - 16 = 0$, $x = \pm 4/5$
3) $(x - 3)^2 = 36$, $x = -1$ or $x = 7$

Completing the Square Exercise (Unit 39)
Write the equation in form $x^2 + bx = d$.

1) $x^2 - 8x = -13$
   $(b/2)^2 = (8/2)^2 = 16$
   $x^2 - 8x + 16 = -13 + 16$
   $(x - 4)^2 = 3$
   $x - 4 = \pm\sqrt{3}$
   $x = 4 \pm\sqrt{3}$
   $x = 5.73$ or $x = 2.27$

2) $x^2 + 4x = -7/2$
   $(b/2)^2 = (4/2)^2 = 4$
   $x^2 + 4x + 4 = -7/2 + 4$
   $(x + 2)^2 = ½$
   $x + 2 = \pm \sqrt{½}$
   $x = -2 \pm \sqrt{½}$
   $x = -1.29$ or $x = -2.71$

Quadratic Equation Exercise (Unit 40)

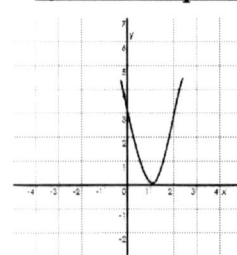

$x = \dfrac{-3 \pm \sqrt{(-6)^2 - 4(3)(3)}}{2(3)}$

$x = 1$

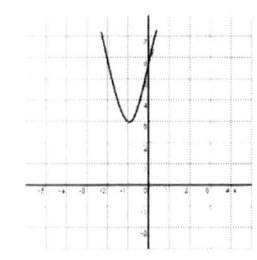

2) $x = \dfrac{-4 \pm \sqrt{(4)^2 - 4(2)(5)}}{2(2)}$

$x = \sqrt{-24}$, There are no real solutions for this equation because $\sqrt{-24}$ is not a real number. This means that the graph never crosses or touches the x-axis.

3) $x = \dfrac{-(-3) \pm \sqrt{(-3)^2 - 4(2)(-1)}}{2(2)}$

$x = \sqrt{17}$; $x \approx 1.178$ or $x \approx -0.28$

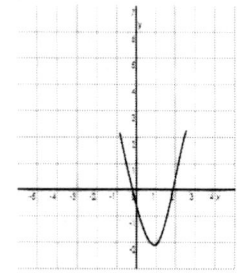

Roots Exercise (Unit 40)
1) There are two solutions
2) There are two solutions
3) There are no solutions
4) There is one solution

Complex Root Exercise (Unit 40)
1) The solutions are $x = i\sqrt{17}$ and $x = -i\sqrt{17}$
2) The solutions are $x = 2 + i$ and $x = 2 - i$
3) The solutions are $x = 5/2 + i\sqrt{5}/2$ and $x = 5/2 - i\sqrt{5}/2$

Test 5 Answers (Unit 41)
1) $x^4y^4, x^3y^2, x^3y^3, xy$; Answer xy
2) $4x^2 - 5x + 9$; Answer Prime polynomial
3) $12x^4 + 17x^2 + 6$; Answer $(4x^2 + 3)(3x^2 + 2)$
4) $2x^2 - 2x - 12$; Answer $2(x + 3)(x - 3)$
5) $x^3 + 6x^2 + 5x + 30$; Answer $(x + 6)(x^2 + 5)$
6) $8a^4b - 18b^3$; Answer $2b(4a^2 + 3b)(2a^2 - 3b)$
7) $x^2 + 4xy - 12y^2$; Answer $(x + 6y)(x - 2y)$
8) $18m^2 - 17r^3$; Answer There are no common factor
9) $x^{10} + 50x^5 + 625$; Answer $(x^5 + 25)^2$
10) $7m^2 + 12m + 1 = 0$; Answer $-6/7 \pm \sqrt{29}/7$
11) $6x^2 + 10x = -3$; Answer $-5/6 \pm \sqrt{7}/6$
12) $x^2 - x = 30$; Answer $-5, 6$
13) $6y^2 + 19y + 10 = 0$; Answer $5/2, 2/3$
14) $x^2 + 4x - 32 = 0$; Answer $-8, 4$
15) 8 inches
16) 120 meters
17) 1024 ft
18) 6ft
19) 4 in
20) 1.5 ft

Index

Absolute Value, 28
AC-Method, 120
Addition, 15, 24
Additive Property, 56
Associative Property, 27
Axis, 86
Base, 51
Binomial Square, 102
Binomial, 93
Cartesian Plan, 86
Circle, 73
Circumference, 73
Coefficient, 94
Commission, 82
Commutative Property, 26
Complete the Square, 129
Complex root, 134
Compound Interest, 84
Cone, 77
Constant, 59, 94
Conversion, 35, 38, 40, 41, 44
Cylinder, 76
Decimal – Addition, 39
Decimal – Division, 41
Decimal – Multiplication, 40
Decimal – Subtraction, 39
Decimal, 39
Degree, 94
Denominator, 31, 35
Diameter, 73
Difference of Squares, 102, 103
Discriminant, 133
Distributive Property, 27
Division, 20, 26
Equations, 47, 59, 63
Equivalent Equations, 56
Estimating, 50
Evaluate, 27
Expanded Notation, 11, 12
Exponents, 51, 49, 94
Expressions, 46
Factor, 48, 110, 112
FOIL- Method, 100
Fraction Notation, 31
Fractions- Adding, 32

Fractions- Multiply, 33
Fractions- Subtracting, 32
Fractions-Divide, 34
Geometric Figure, 70
Greatest Common Factor, 111, 112
Grouping, 114
Imaginary, 134
Improper Fraction, 35
Inequalities, 62, 63
Integer, 13
Intercept, 89, 90
Irrational Number, 13
Laws of Operation, 24
Least Common Denominator, 31
Like Terms, 60, 94
Line, 70
Linear Equation – See Equations, 59
Long Division, 22
Long Multiplication, 19
Mixed Numerals, 35
Mixed Numerals-Adding, 36
Mixed Numerals-Dividing, 37
Mixed Numerals-Multiplying, 37
Mixed Numerals-Subtracting, 36
Monomial, 93
Multiplication, 18, 19, 25
Multiplicative Property, 56, 57
Natural Number, 13
Negative Exponent, 51
Negative Numbers, 23
Numerator, 31
Opposite, 23, 96
Order of Operation, 26, 140
Ordered Pairs, 86, 88
Percentage, 80, 81
Perfect Squares see Binomial Square
Point of Origination, 86
Polynomial, 93
Polynomial-Adding, 96
Polynomial-Dividing, 105
Polynomial-Multiplying, 98, 104
Polynomial-Subtracting, 97
Power Rule, 53
Prime, 41, 110, 118, 130
Product Rule, 52

Product, 19
Proper Fraction, 35
Proportional, 78
Pythagoras Theorem, 126
Quadratic Equation, 124, 130, 133
Quadratic Formula, 130
Quotient Rule, 52
Quotient, 13, 21
Radius, 73
Rate, 78
Ratio, 78
Rational Number, 13
Real Number, 13, 26
Rectangle, 71
Right Triangle, 123
Rounding 49
Rules of Operation, 28
Sales Tax, 82
Scientific Notation, 54
Segment, 70
Simple Interest, 84
Simplify, 27
Sphere, 76
Square Root Property, 128
Square Root, 128
Square, 72
Standard Notation, 11, 12
Subtraction, 17, 26
Surface Area, 75
Term, 63, 94
Trial & Error, 115
Triangle, 70
Trinomial, 93
Variable(s), 46, 94
Volume, 76
Whole Numbers, 10, 13
Zero Property, 124

CPSIA information can be obtained
at www.ICGtesting.com
Printed in the USA
LVOW09s1639200317
527827LV00009B/788/P

9 781479 208074